THE LITTLE BOOK OF BIG MANAGEMENT WISDOM

James McGrath

THE LITTLE BOOK OF BIG MANAGEMENT WISDOM

90 IMPORTANT QUOTES AND HOW TO USE THEM IN BUSINESS

PEARSON

Harlow, England • London • New York • Boston • San Francisco • Toronto • Sydney
Auckland • Singapore • Hong Kong • Tokyo • Seoul • Taipei • New Delhi
Cape Town • São Paulo • Mexico City • Madrid • Amsterdam • Munich • Paris • Milan

Pearson Education Limited
Edinburgh Gate
Harlow CM20 2JE
United Kingdom
Tel: +44 (0)1279 623623
Web: www.pearson.com/uk

First published 2017 (print and electronic)

ISBN: 978-1-292-14843-4 (print)
        978-1-292-14844-1 (PDF)
        978-1-292-14845-8 (ePub)

British Library Cataloguing-in-Publication Data
A catalogue record for the print edition is available from the British Library

Library of Congress Cataloging-in-Publication Data
A catalog record for the print edition is available from the Library of Congress

10 9 8 7 6 5 4 3 2 1
20 19 18 17 16

Cover design by Nick Redeyoff

Print edition typeset in Helvetica Neue LT W1G 9.5 by SPi Global
Printed in Great Britain by Ashford Colour Press Ltd

NOTE THAT ANY PAGE CROSS REFERENCES REFER TO THE PRINT EDITION

For Tallulah and Finbar

CONTENTS

SECTION 3 MANAGING PEOPLE AND TEAMS 49

SECTION 4 LEADERSHIP 77

ABOUT THE AUTHOR

James McGrath is a qualified accountant with over 25 years' experience of working in the public and private sectors as an accountant, auditor, financial controller and management consultant.

He joined the University of Central England in 1998 where he was the Course Director for the MA in Education and Professional Development. He studied for his doctorate at The University of Birmingham and wrote his doctoral thesis on management and leadership in education.

He has co-written five non-fiction books including *The Little Book of Big Management Theories* which won the 2015 CMI Management Book of the Year Award: Practical Manager Category. This is his third solo book.

In addition, James has published the first two novels in his planned Handsworth Quartet – *A Death in Winter: 1963* and *A Death in Spring: 1968*. He plans to publish the final two books in the quartet during 2017.

ACKNOWLEDGEMENTS

I'd like to thank my editor Eloise Cook for suggesting the idea for this book and the support she has given throughout the writing process. I'd also like to thank Priyadharshini Dhanagopal for her help and understanding during the production stage. We Luddites need a bit of help and understanding sometimes.

INTRODUCTION

This book isn't about theories or models; it's about practical management insights from people who know what they are talking about. Yes, theories and models are important. They can open a manager's mind to a wide range of new ideas and ways of thinking. However, long before they became popular, there were aphorisms, sayings and quotations that well-known managers such as Henry Ford and politicians like Lincoln had made famous. Such quotations captured fundamental truths about business and management. Later, managers, leaders and commentators added to this rich treasure of succinct nuggets of management wisdom. This book explores 90 such pearls of wisdom and how to apply in practice the insights they contain.

CHOICE OF QUOTATIONS

Inevitably, there is an element of personal bias in the quotations I've chosen. However, I've tried to minimise this: otherwise you might have had 90 quotations from Peter Drucker! To be eligible for inclusion, all quotations used had to:

- have been made by a well-known person, usually a famous manager/entrepreneur, management expert, military or political leader;
- be based upon either research or many years' experience working in the field;
- be relevant to the needs of today's managers;
- be sufficiently profound/complex to be of value to today's busy managers.

My aim was to select a range of quotations that were both interesting and useful. Don't be put off by the apparent age of some of the quotations: wisdom existed before the technological revolution and human nature hasn't changed in millennia.

A list of contributors can be found on page 231 along with the number of quotations I've used from each person.

WHAT THIS BOOK WILL DO FOR YOU
The Little Book of Big Management Wisdom will:

- extend and deepen your understanding of a wide range of management issues;

- help you to better understand your attitude to life and work;
- help you to recognise what motivates you and your staff;
- provide you with insights into a wide range of practical management issues that many theories and models don't deal with;
- improve your effectiveness as a manager;
- prepare you for promotion and increase your earning power.

KEEPING IT SHORT, SHARP AND CLEAR

I recognise that managers are busy people. You don't have the time to plough through pages of text to reach the essential message. For that reason the book does not discuss the finer implications of some of the quotations. Instead, it's succinct and punchy with all non-essential material eliminated. What you are left with are 90 lessons in management wisdom, which, if understood and applied, will improve your performance.

Eighty-two of the quotations are outlined and guidance given in a series of two-page entries and eight (see Section 11) are dealt with in a single page. This means that in less than five minutes you can read, understand and be ready to apply the advice given. All you need to supply is the will and self-confidence to give it a try.

In only one respect have I departed from the above principle of brevity. Because you are likely to dip in and out of this book rather than read it from cover to cover, there are a few entries where the same advice has to be repeated, e.g. 'Get to know and understand your staff'.

The book is intended for senior, middle and junior managers and anyone who aspires to be a manager. What each person takes from the book will differ dependent upon their seniority and experience. Some of the advice may seem irrelevant to a junior manager but may open new avenues of thinking for a middle or senior manager. Ambitious young managers, who want to be on the board by the age of 30, will find that it enhances their thinking and analytical skills when faced with a problem.

HOW THE BOOK IS ORGANISED

The book is divided into 11 sections. Inevitably, in a book of this kind, many quotations could appear in more than one section. So don't assume that you can apply the information given in only one area. For example, Drucker's views on the need to make and retain a customer appears in Section 1 – Managing a successful business – but could just as easily have been included in Section 10 – Turning customers into partners.

Each of the 90 entries contains 4 sections:

- When to use the quotation.
- The quotation and, where required, a brief comment on it.
- How to use it to improve your professional practice.
- Questions to ask yourself.

Any words that I have added to a quotation, to make the meaning clearer, are shown in brackets.

From each of the first ten sections I have nominated one quotation for inclusion in the The Top Ten management wisdom quotations. The intention is to identify the ten great management insights that every manager should commit to memory. But, I also hope that the list will encourage you to identify your own favourites and get you thinking about which ten you would find most useful in your unique situation.

AND FINALLY . . .

I'd like to wish you every success with your career and hope you enjoy the book. If you have any comments you'd like to make about the book, please leave a review on www.amazon.co.uk, or a comment on either my Amazon Author's Page or on my blog www.goodreads.com

James McGrath
July 2016

HOW TO GET THE MOST OUT OF THIS BOOK

I f you are serious about trying to apply some of the insights contained in this book, then I suggest you quickly review the entire book. Once you have an idea of its contents, identify a problem that you have and select the entry that you think is most likely to resolve it. Read the entry again and implement the approach suggested. You don't have to follow every suggestion in an entry. You may also decide to combine one or two entries in order to meet your unique requirement. This amend, mix and match approach is the correct strategy to adopt when using this book.

In order to increase your learning, annotate the book as you go along. Note which ideas could be applied with no amendments and those which you might be able to use if you changed the advice given or combined two or more entries.

Once you have actually tried to implement an idea, jot down a few short notes about how well or badly your intervention went; what you would do differently next time in a similar situation; which other ideas you could have used but didn't. By reflecting on both your successes and failures, you are embedding knowledge in your brain which you'll be able to access in the future when required. Do this and you'll quickly turn this book into a learning journal which you can refer to time and again.

Feel free to reject certain entries that you don't like/agree with but, before you do so, identify what it is about the idea that you dislike. If you tried to apply a similar approach in the past and things went badly, ask yourself, 'Was it the idea or how I used it that was the problem?'

SECTION 1

MANAGING A SUCCESSFUL BUSINESS

INTRODUCTION

This book is intended for junior, middle and senior managers and those that aspire to be a manager. Therefore, many of you may be tempted to skip this section as you don't run the business you are employed in. That would be a mistake. As a middle or junior manager, you run a team, section or department. That is your business and the principles outlined in this section are just as applicable to your domain as to the entire organisation. For example, your department or section may contribute to the organisation's cash-flow problems (see Quotation 4) or failure to control costs (see Quotation 5).

There are three categories of entries in this section. Quotations:

- 1 and 2 deal with the essential prerequisites that any business needs if it is to succeed, namely customers and a competitive advantage.
- 3 to 8 are concerned with the basics of running any business.
- 9 and 10 consider some of the reasons businesses decline and fail and suggest ways to minimise these risks.

Some of the entries in this section talk about customers. Many managers claim that they don't have any customers. They say things like, 'I'm just the accountant or purchasing manager. I don't sell anything.' This misses a vital point. Just because you provide an internal service to colleagues does not mean that you have no customers. The colleagues who receive and use your reports or use the materials you purchase are your customers. You need to treat them as such. Especially as they have greater access to the powers that be within the organisation than external customers. Therefore, unless you want complaints and criticisms to quickly reach the ears of your boss, you need to treat them as valued customers.

Finally, it's worth remembering that, if you are in business just to make money, it will be a poor business. The really big bucks are made by people who love the job they do and just use money to keep score.

QUOTATION 1 PETER DRUCKER ON WHY CUSTOMERS ARE MORE IMPORTANT THAN PROFITS (TOP TEN ENTRY)

Use this to keep you focused on what's most important in any business – the customer.

Ask most people what the primary purpose of a business is and they'll say either, 'To make a profit' or 'To maximise profits'. Peter Drucker (1909–2005), perhaps the only true genius that the discipline of management has produced, challenges this view. He argues that:

> A business exists to create [and retain] a customer.
>
> **Peter Drucker**

Despite the need to win and retain customers, it is still the case that far too many organisations see customers, and their complaints, as annoying distractions from the real work of the organisation. The truth is that there are only two enterprises that can treat their customers with contempt and still prosper – drug dealing and football clubs.

WHAT TO DO

- Unless you have already done so, re-orientate your thinking. Stop obsessing over profits and start to think about how you can improve the service you offer customers. Satisfied customers will tell their friends about you. Dissatisfied customers will tell everyone!
- Treat existing customers as the valuable assets they are and not the annoying nuisance that many staff consider them to be.
- Train all your staff to recognise that customers are the organisation's most precious assets and should be treated as such. This applies as much to the accounting staff chasing a debt as the sales staff pushing a new product.
- The main reason customers change suppliers is because they feel underappreciated and exploited. This is hardly surprising if you consistently offer new customers better deals than you do to existing customers. No one wants to feel exploited. Never offer better deals to

new customers than those offered to existing customers – regardless of what your marketing team says about expanding market share.

- Keep in touch with customers. Use email, phone, newsletters and personal visits to improve and maintain your relationship. On these occasions don't try to sell anything. Just try to create a relationship of trust.

- To build trust, always keep your word. Don't renege on a deal or a promise even if it means you lose money. If you fail to deliver on your word you'll lose the person's trust and probably their custom.

- Be frank with customers. If there's a problem or a delay, tell them. If you can't answer a question, don't invent one. Tell them you don't know but that you'll find out and get back to them.

- Listen to what customers say. Use their feedback to improve existing products and as a source of ideas for new and/or improved products.

- In particular, pay attention to what your customers say about your competitors. Avoid the mistakes your competitors make and don't hesitate to steal their good ideas and practice. In particular, pick up any intelligence you can about new or improved products that your competition are developing and feed it back to your organisation.

- Reward customer loyalty and prompt payment by offering selected customers higher discounts, better payment terms, special deals and invitations to special events.

QUESTIONS TO ASK

- When was the last time I phoned, or met with, a customer to discuss how I could improve the service they receive without trying to sell them something?

- What percentage of complaints do we resolve on first contact with a customer?

QUOTATION 2

JACK WALSH ON THE NEED FOR A COMPETITIVE ADVANTAGE

Use this to determine whether your business is likely to be successful.

Jack Walsh (b. 1935) was the highly successful CEO of General Electric between 1981 and 2001. He gave the following advice to any entrepreneur or executive thinking of entering a new market or business.

> If you don't have a competitive advantage, don't compete.
>
> **Jack Walsh**

Managers are often poor at identifying the competitive strengths and weaknesses in their organisation. Generally, the myopia increases with seniority, but it's present throughout the organisation. For example, in every SWOT analysis that I've ever been involved in, it has been claimed that one of the organisation's great strengths is 'a well-trained and committed workforce'. The statement may be true, but, unless your staff are better than those employed by all your competitors, it doesn't give you a competitive advantage. At best it means you are competing on a level playing field.

Who has the competitive advantage?

WHAT TO DO

- Identify any existing competitive advantages that your organisation enjoys or could achieve if changes were made to current operations. Only in the smallest organisations will you be able to do this on your own. Therefore, pull together a small team of people from different levels and departments in the organisation.
- Don't pack the team with managers. Look for smart people who work with your customers and know what the competition is doing on the street.

- Without divulging what new products or business you are thinking about acquiring, ask the team to identify the strengths that exist in the organisation. Get as many ideas out as you can. List them on Post-it Notes, arrange them under broad categories and stick them on the wall.

- When the list is complete, introduce the new product or idea into the discussion and remove from the list those strengths that will have no effect on the new business or product. Ask the team to identify any strengths that apply specifically to the new product or business that have not been listed. What you now have is a list of items that you/ your organisation do/does well.

- But that does not mean that they provide you with a competitive advantage. You need to take each strength and test it against your strongest competitor in that area. For example, you identify the following possible competitive advantages: price, quality, brand recognition, excellent technology and customer service. Compare each strength against the current competitor who is leader in that field using benchmarking (see Quotation 82).

- You don't have to achieve a competitive advantage in each area; you just need an edge in one or two areas that you can exploit. For example, Apple enjoys a competitive advantage for its design and brand image that few organisations can touch.

- Small companies can usually compete on speed, personal attention and cost.

- If you have a totally new product, the question is: can you make it at a price the customer is willing to pay?

QUESTIONS TO ASK

- How much effort are you willing to put into establishing the new product or business?
- How resilient is each of the competitive advantages identified? Will competitors be able to quickly overcome them?

QUOTATION 3
MARVIN BOWER ON WHY MORE COHESION AND LESS HIERARCHY IS REQUIRED IN ORGANISATIONS

Use this to help you break down hierarchical structures and improve organisational cohesion.

Marvin Bower (1903–2003) was an American business theorist, management consultant and the CEO of management consultants McKinsey and Co. He argued that to improve organisational performance:

> More cohesion is needed rather than [more] hierarchy.
>
> [What is required is] a network of leaders.
>
> **Marvin Bower**

It can be argued that the move towards flatter structures during the late 1980s and 1990s has created fewer levels of management within many organisations. However, that does not mean that organisations are any less hierarchal than what existed 40 years ago. Power and control still flow from the top, usually in the form of a series of stultifying instructions, targets and objectives which demotivate, rather than energise, staff. Too often, achievement of the target becomes more important than doing a good job or satisfying the customers.

WHAT TO DO

- To improve cohesion, seek to increase formal and informal channels of leadership within the organisation. Unlike managers, leaders do not require positional power to exercise influence. People respond to them because they trust the leader and want to respond to their urgings. This means that leaders can be found at every level in the organisation, from level one supervisors to board members.

- Identify who the staff in your organisation look to for both formal and informal leadership. Within any office or production unit there will be one or more leaders whom staff look to for advice and guidance. They may be a member of staff, a supervisor or, possibly, a manager. These are the people that you want to work through to achieve greater cohesion and co-ordination without the need to rely on hierarchical power exercised by a chosen few.

- Use the following typology of dispersed leadership to decide how much power you wish to devolve to the people identified:
  - **Delegated:** You retain ultimate power, but check whether the person is willing and able to undertake specified work and offer support when it's requested (see Quotation 51).
  - **Distributed:** You distribute power to those who already hold a formal management position in the organisation and advise them to encourage, not stifle, collaboration and joint working.
  - **Democratic within existing structures:** You ask others for their opinions and encourage collaboration and joint decision making.
  - **Democratic – challenging existing structures:** You allow nominated leaders within the organisation to challenge existing power structures and practices and to take on the responsibility for changing them.
  - **Dispersed:** You encourage the emergence of leaders in informal and spontaneous ways that may not be planned or even approved by you.
- In seeking dispersed leadership, you are feeding into people's desire to take responsibility for their work and to act as they see fit within reasonable limits.
- Effectively, you want to encourage managers and staff to take greater responsibility for their work, improve communication with colleagues and management and co-ordinate their actions with other teams and departments.
- Encouraging dispersed leadership is not the same as abrogating responsibility. You still have to maintain an overview of what is going on in your department or organisation and step in when required. But, if you follow the advice of Warren Buffet on recruitment of staff (see Quotation 25), such occasions will be few and far between.

QUESTIONS TO ASK

- Does the organisation's culture allow for aspects of dispersed leadership? If not, can I change the culture (see Quotation 63)?
- How comfortable am I with the concept of dispersed leadership? What are my concerns?

QUOTATION 4 HAROLD GENEEN ON WHY CASH IS KING

Use this to remind you that cash flow is more important than profits.

Harold Geneen (1910–97), was President of the ITT Corporation of America. In a long and distinguished career, he came to recognise the pre-eminent importance of cash to any organisation:

> The only unforgivable sin in business is to run out of cash.
>
> **Harold Geneen**

It is surprising how many experienced managers fail to understand the difference between cash and profit. It is entirely possible to have cash in the bank but make a loss. It's also possible to have very little cash but be raking in large profits.

For example, a company's sales may be rocketing. However, if the organisation is paying its suppliers every 30 days while its customers are taking 50 days plus to settle their accounts, it'll quickly run out of cash and end up insolvent because of overtrading.

Insolvency occurs when an organisation has insufficient cash to pay its debts as they fall due. Insolvency can be a temporary affair lasting just a few days or weeks as the organisation waits for a large payment. In such cases, it's likely that you'll be able to arrange a loan or overdraft from your bank. Alternatively, it can be an early warning sign that things are going downhill. **It is illegal to continue trading if you are insolvent.** That is why cash is, and always will be, king.

WHAT TO DO

- Constantly look out for signs of insolvency: for example, suppliers complaining that they haven't received payment or that payments are delayed, delays in purchasing essential goods or materials and, most telling of all, any delays in the payment of wages or salaries.
- Insist on receiving a cash-flow report from your accountant, at least monthly, which shows the projected cash flows for the following three months. Recognise that the figures for the first month are likely to be fairly accurate but thereafter the level of accuracy decreases.

- If you are suffering from cash-flow problems, insist on a weekly report covering the next 12 weeks.
- Mere receipt of the report will not improve your cash-flow position. You have to take corrective action. Working with your accountant and those responsible for sales, purchases and credit control, identify where the problems lie and take remedial action.
- Examine the aged debtors list first. Develop a strategy for collecting all debts that are in excess of your normal terms and conditions or where an extension has been negotiated by the customer.
- Possible problems include:
  - Allowing sales to continue trading with slow payers and/or those who have a poor credit rating.
  - Granting buyers unsustainable credit terms. Once in a blue moon you might extend the payment date to help out a valuable customer to, say, 60 days. But you can't offer such generous terms as a matter of policy if you are required to pay your debtors within 30 days.
  - Failure to supply managers with an aged debtors report and to require them to take corrective action. This may mean refusing to sell any further goods to a customer until they clear or reduce their debts.
  - Failure to issue sales invoices the same day as goods are despatched.

QUESTIONS TO ASK

- Do I see cash-flow problems as something that the accountant is responsible for?
- Do I know the effect that the accountant's actions have on my customers/suppliers?

QUOTATION 5

ANDREW CARNEGIE ON TAKING CARE OF THE PENNIES

Use this to remind you of the need to control costs.

The old saying, 'Take care of the pennies and the pounds will take care of themselves', was reformulated by the great Scottish American businessman Andrew Carnegie (1835–1919) for use by managers:

> Watch the costs and the profits will take care of themselves.
>
> **Andrew Carnegie**

Profits   Costs

Perhaps the best example of paying attention to the little things and achieving huge rewards is Masaaki Imai's approach to quality. His Kaizen model suggests that instead of improving one facet of production by 10 per cent in an effort to improve quality, managers should attempt to improve all aspects by just 1 per cent. The overall improvement will be many times greater than the former approach.

It is the same with expenditure. It's easier to save £100 on each of 1,000 activities than £100,000 on 1 activity.

WHAT TO DO

■ To develop a Kaizen-inspired approach to expenditure you need to act as an exemplar to all your staff. This means walking the talk. Be consistent in your actions and show your determination to follow this approach, even when others are demanding that you cut expenditure by 15 per cent from the training and advertising budgets immediately. In the long run, such arbitrary cuts damage the organisation's ability to grow.

- Start by getting out of your office and seeing what is actually going on in offices and on the shop floor. This is management by walking about and does not require you to undertake a detailed analysis of what's happening: that can come later, if required. It's concerned with looking at what people are doing. As an informed, intelligent and critical observer, you'll see plenty of things that strike you as odd or inefficient; make a note of them.

- Talk to the staff, don't interrogate them. Ask them about the problems they face and what they would do to improve processes and practices. Specifically ask them for their ideas on how costs could be reduced. Stress that you're interested in shaving costs, not cutting jobs or whole processes.

- Back in your office, list the ideas identified and, in conjunction with the relevant members of staff, identify which are likely to produce actual savings. Don't be greedy. Look for small, easy-to-implement savings that will have a quick impact and show staff that savings can be made without impacting on staffing levels or salaries.

- Always recognise good suggestions and seek to reward the person who made it. Don't take credit for your staff's ideas. If you do, ideas will dry up. You'll get the credit for increased profits: that should be enough for you.

- This approach can't be a one-off exercise; it is a continuous process which you must commit to indefinitely.

- Share at least a proportion of the savings with the staff affected.

- A windfall benefit of this approach is that staff will become more motivated because they will feel that their views are being listened to (see Quotation 45).

QUESTIONS TO ASK

- Do I have the determination and self-discipline to adopt this approach indefinitely?

- Where are the pennies that I could save in my work?

QUOTATION 6   SAM WALTON ON WHY YOU SHOULD IGNORE CONVENTIONAL WISDOM

Use this to remind you that today's conventional wisdom was once radical and untried.

Sam Walton (1918–92) was an American businessman and entrepreneur who founded the retailer Walmart. A believer in the unconventional, his motto was:

> Swim upstream. Go the other way. Ignore conventional wisdom.
>
> **Sam Walton**

Sam Walton believed that by swimming against the tide it's possible to identify both small and big ideas, which can be exploited to improve organisational practice and performance.

WHAT TO DO

- Generating new ideas is not easy. Fortunately, a technique known as SCAMPER can be invaluable. Select a small team of between three and six people to assist you with your search for new ideas. Choose people from different disciplines and levels within the organisation.
- At your first meeting, explain how the SCAMPER process takes an existing product, service or process and subjects it to a review intended to improve or replace what currently exists.
- As a warm-up exercise, ask the group to come up with at least 20 different uses for a balloon or table fork. Both items can generate some interesting ideas which will get the group relaxed and laughing and, of course, people are more creative when they are relaxed.
- Using the SCAMPER search for new ideas, ask whether we can:
  - **Substitute:** existing components, machines or human resources to improve the product.
  - **Combine:** one or more of the products functions. Reconfigure how we use the human and material resources to improve how people see the product and its uses.
  - **Adapt:** the product for use in a different context. Thanks to the success of *50 Shades of Grey* manufacturers of handcuffs now

enjoy a whole new market, and all they had to add to their basic
product was a fluffy covering (or so I'm told).

- **Modify:** the size, shape, feel, texture, smell or functionality of the
product. Which existing features could be enhanced to create more
value in the product and make it more attractive to customers?
- **Find another use for the product:** You only have to think about
the multiple uses that simple everyday objects, such as a brick or
paperclip, can be put to realise that we seldom exploit all the uses
of even common products.
- **Eliminate any elements:** of the product, process or change and
simplify it without adversely affecting its effectiveness or appeal to
customers. For example, mobile-phone manufacturers now realise
that there is a market for chunky phones with big buttons and
limited functionality for the older consumer.
- **Reverse:** or invert long-held ideas about how the product is made
or marketed. For example, Roberts Radio has made a huge success
out of housing a range of DAB radios in 1950s/60s-style cabinets.

- Once you have identified a series of possible changes, evaluate each
in terms of cost/return and, if they look like a financial goer, run some
small-scale tests as to their practicality.
- If your test results look good, take your best ideas to senior management for
approval/implementation and be prepared to rebut criticisms of your ideas.

QUESTIONS TO ASK

- Whose support do I need to implement the ideas generated?
- Who is likely to oppose the ideas generated? What do I need to do to
minimise their influence on decision makers?

QUOTATION 7 JEFF BOZOS ON TWO WAYS TO EXPAND YOUR BUSINESS

Use this when considering your growth strategy for your team or organisation.

Jeff Bozos (b. 1964), founder and CEO of Amazon, started Amazon in his garage. From there, it has become a multi national behemoth in less than 25 years. It is, therefore, probably worthwhile listening to what he has to say about how to grow an organisation:

> There are two ways to expand your business. Take inventory of what you are good at and extend out from your skills. Or determine what your customers need and work backwards, even if that means learning new skills.
>
> **Jeff Bozos**

WHAT TO DO

- Any decision about expanding your current operation is, by nature, a strategic decision that will require planning. Therefore, review the contents of section 8 and select the information that will be most useful to you in your unique situation.

- Recognise that what Jeff Bozos offers is not a binary choice. You can combine aspects of both. In the early days of a business you may be so busy that there is no time for you or your staff to learn new skills. This means that growth will have to be a product of your existing skills.

- Use early expansion efforts as an opportunity to hone the organisation's existing skills. Look for ways to build on and improve what you currently do. Learn from the mistakes you made during the early days of the business: for example, overtrading. And don't repeat them (see Quotation 5).

- If you decide to base your expansion on what the customers want, then start by confirming what they want. This is so obvious that many organisations fail to do it. Even when you ask people directly what they want, there is often a gap between what they say and what they actually want. There is also the issue that people don't know what they want until they see it. For example, there was no great clamour for portable personal stereos until Akio Morita invented the Sony Walkman. Is it any wonder that so many organisations end up providing goods and services that *they think* customers want rather than what customers *actually want?*

■ To find out what people really, really want will require a mixture of professional market research and information already held in your organisation by front-line staff. Sales reps and other staff who deal with customers on a daily basis have a vast fund of knowledge about what customers want, like and dislike. Bring these people together in small focus groups and ask them open-ended questions which will allow discussion and debate. The data collected will be far richer than most market surveys provide, but will require careful analysis.

■ Once you've established what your customers want, undertake a training needs analysis for each member of staff. Start by recording what skills each person has and their level of proficiency. Compare this to the skills and knowledge that that are required to successfully implement the expansion plan. The difference between the two is the skills gap that you need to close through training and development.

QUESTIONS TO ASK

■ When was the last time that I attended a training session, even with my staff?

■ Do I see training and development as an investment in the organisation's future or a cost?

QUOTATION 8 PHILIP KOTLER ON CREATING MARKETS

Use this to help you search for new markets.

Philip Kotler (b. 1931) is an American author and consultant who has written over 50 books on marketing. He is also Professor of International Marketing at the Kellogg School of Management at Northwestern University, Illinois. He suggests that:

> Good companies will meet needs. Great companies will create markets.
>
> **Philip Kotler**

An example of how to create a market was provided by John Paul Getty who famously established a string of petrol stations across America at a time when motoring was reserved for the very rich. In doing so, he helped create the conditions in which the modern car industry could develop and, in turn, a market for his own oil refining waste product – gasoline. Sheer genius.

WHAT TO DO

- Read Quotation 6 for ways in which you can identify a new or improved products which may develop into a new market.

- W. Chan Kim and Renée Mauborgne's Blue Ocean Model differentiates between what they call Red and Blue Ocean Strategies (BOS). The model doesn't tell you how to create a new market/ industry, rather it provides a valuable way of thinking about where an organisation should position itself vis-à-vis their competition, e.g.

Red Ocean Strategy is concerned with existing markets. Management . . .	Blue Ocean Strategy is concerned with new markets. Management . . .
■ Concentrates on beating the competition in existing markets.	■ Looks to identify new market places free of competitors.
■ Looks to maximise existing demand.	■ Seeks to identify, create and exploit new demand.
■ Believes that there is a trade-off between value and cost and aligns its strategy accordingly.	■ Does not believe that there is a trade-off between value and cost.

Red Ocean Strategy is concerned with existing markets. Management . . .	*Blue Ocean Strategy is concerned with new markets. Management . . .*
■ Thinks that BOS is all about new technology.	■ Does not think that BOS is concerned solely with new technology. Traditional technology can also supply opportunities. ■ Aligns the organisation's culture, strategy, processes and activities around the idea of product differentiation and low cost.

- When thinking about new markets you and/or your board must decide which industry-wide standards:
  - can be ignored/eliminated;
  - should be reduced below the current accepted norm in the industry;
  - should be raised above the current accepted norm in the industry;
  - can be created in the industry for the first time and offered to customers.
- When considering the above questions, it's essential that customer value drives the discussion not how the competition are going to react. In your blue ocean there will be no competitors if you get it right (at least initially).
- Start by identifying potential blue oceans in which the risks are minimised. What you are doing is risky enough without operating in a risky sector.
- Think in big-picture terms.
- Ignore current demand. You are looking for unmet demands, which was what John Paul Getty did.
- Focus on building a strong business model that will ensure long-term profit. Work up the costs and cash flows of everything in as much detail as possible.
- To minimise opposition, involve staff when planning and ensure that you maintain great communication with them at all times (see Quotation 66).

QUESTIONS TO ASK

- Am I enough of a risk taker to try and establish a new market?
- Who do I need to get onside before I start?

LAURENCE J. PETER ON WHY PEOPLE RISE TO THE LEVEL OF THEIR OWN INCOMPETENCE

Use this to remind you of the need to review the performance of all staff.

The Peter Principle was devised by Laurence J. Peter (1919–90), a Canadian educator and hierarchiologist who was interested in organisation structures and hierarchies. His work often is dismissed as something of a joke, but it contains valuable insights into the nature of hierarchal organisations. The most famous of which is that:

> In a hierarchy every employee rises to the level of their own incompetence.
>
> **Laurence J. Peter**

People often assume that the principle cannot be correct because it would mean that all managers in an organisation are incompetent and would, therefore, quickly go out of business. Such an interpretation is incorrect. Peter recognises that many managers operate at a level below their own incompetence and others will never reach it. Therefore, the organisation continues to prosper. It is when key posts are occupied by people who have risen to the level of their own incompetence that an organisation is in real trouble.

WHAT TO DO

- You can never be sure that an appointment or a promotion will be successful. Therefore, protect yourself by including in contracts a probationary period during which the contract can be terminated.
- In order to ensure that your own staff continue to apply for promotion, include in the contract a provision for the person to return to their previous post or one of equivalent pay and status.
- Before deciding that an appointment isn't working, undertake a review of the person's performance, which takes into account their inexperience in the new post. This review should be conducted before the end of the person's probationary period. This will provide time for

corrective action to be taken, including providing additional training or mentoring.

■ Don't allow the transfer from probationer to permanent staff to be rubber-stamped. It should be treated as a significant financial decision with cumulative costs running into hundreds of thousands of pounds.

■ Allow high-performing staff to remain in their current post if they wish to and reward them for their outstanding performance. Not everyone wants to be promoted. Many people enjoy what they are doing and are intelligent enough to realise that, even if they could make a success of their new job, it would not provide them with the job satisfaction or work–life balance that they want.

■ Recognise that interviews are a very poor way of selecting staff, as the skills required to impress in an interview are not those required to do any job on a day-to-day basis. Use the advice given by Warren Buffet to improve your chances of appointing a star performer (see Quotation 25).

■ Remember, ever since the post of village idiot was abolished, some people reach the level of their own incompetence when given responsibility for opening the post. Often these people are convinced that they are brilliant and should be running the place. It's best to get rid of them as soon as possible.

QUESTIONS TO ASK

■ Have I reached the level of my own incompetence? Which of my staff have reached the level of their own incompetence?

■ Do I really want to be promoted or do I apply for promotions because people expect me to do so?

QUOTATION 10

WARREN BENNIS ON WHY FAILING ORGANISATIONS NEED LEADERSHIP NOT MORE MANAGEMENT

Use this to remind you of the need to let go and empower others.

Warren Bennis (1925–2015) was a management consultant, writer and academic who pioneered the comparatively new field of leadership studies. In both his research and consultation work he observed that:

> Failing organisations are usually over-managed and under-led.
>
> **Warren Bennis**

Bennis's argument is that too many organisations micro-manage their staff and in doing so crush their enthusiasm and their willingness to act independently. When things start to go wrong, management assumes that the answer is even greater control of staff and additional policies and procedure, when what is actually required is to give staff the discretion and power to sort problems out at their level. After all, they understand their problems and how to correct them better than senior management. All they need is the freedom to do so (see Quotation 45).

WHAT TO DO

- Organisations fail because they are too slow to react to changing circumstances and emerging threats. To survive, you need a workforce that is flexible and willing to make decisions without referring every little issue up the chain of command.
- Flexible, autonomous staff are not created overnight. They have to be grown in the right environment. Follow the advice of Andrew S. Grove (see Quotation 65) and look to manage your staff and organisation on the basis of clearly defined principles and precepts rather than detailed instructions. If you do this, then staff will be programmed already to respond proactively to emerging threats and will feel confident enough to take the necessary decisions.

- Recognise that you can't do everything or foresee every eventuality. Appoint good people (see Quotation 27) and then let them get on with their job. Don't interfere unnecessarily. What you are aiming to create is an organisation in which you provide the framework within which people exercise their discretion and only come to you when they are worried or realise that the decision is outside their area of discretion.
- By adopting this approach, you are empowering your staff to lead and decide how best to react to issues and events on the ground. This negates the need for every possible eventuality to be covered by a process or procedure and frees up staff to respond to the problem they are facing immediately with imagination and ingenuity.

QUESTIONS TO ASK

- Am I a control freak? Do my staff think I'm a control freak?
- Do I get involved in too many detailed decisions/discussions?

CONCLUSION

The Top Ten entry from this section is:

> A business exists to create [and retain] a customer.
>
> **Peter Drucker**

I chose Drucker's definition of what an organisation's aim is for two reasons.

First, I'm fed up with people repeating the age-old mantra that the purpose of a business is to maximise profits. To maximise profits an organisation has to be willing to maximise risk. I don't see too many shareholders or managers signing up for such a terrifying ride. What shareholders and managers want is a reasonable return on investment in return for taking low or minimal risks. A case of producing satisfactory rather than sensational profits.

Second, it reminds us all that before profits can be earned a customer must be won. There is no chicken and egg situation here. Without customers there are no profits.

ONE LESSON TO TAKE AWAY

The quotations discussed in this section cover a wide range of issues. If you are from a specific professional discipline, you may find it hard to see the relevance of some of them. That's understandable. However, if you want to reach the top, you need to stop thinking like an accountant, engineer or human resource manager and start thinking like a general manager.

Stop viewing your organisation through the single lens of your own background and instead view it on a full Imax screen in all its complex detail and interrelations. A problem on the factory floor caused by an out-of-date machine is not just an engineering problem: it also has financial implications (how much will it cost to replace?) and human resource issues (will we need as many people to run the new machine as the old?).

SECTION 2

MANAGING YOURSELF AND YOUR CAREER

INTRODUCTION

Most people don't have a career, they have a job. They don't think about what they do as their life's work. Instead they see their job as the means by which they pay their bills and finance their real interests. There is nothing wrong with this. Not everyone wants to devote the time and energy required to build a career.

For those that do want to build a career, this chapter contains a wealth of wisdom that will both inspire and guide you throughout your career. The section is structured as follows. Quotations:

- 11 to 15 are all about you and what you bring or need to bring to the table.
- 16 to 18 outline three strategies you must adopt if you are going to be a successful manager.
- 19 and 20 are about deciding how much time you are willing to devote to your career and how best to manage this finite resource.

Two quotations that you won't find in this section, but that I think are amongst my favourites, were made by two very different giants of culture. Five hundred years ago, Michelangelo suggested that:

> The greatest danger for most of us is not that our aim is too high and we miss, but that is too low and we reach it.
>
> **Michelangelo**

Too often, we place arbitrary limits on ourselves, which stops us achieving all that we could. It's more fulfilling to aim high and fall short by an inch than to aim low and hit your target. Why? Because you will know that you gave it your best shot. You didn't play it safe and, even though you may have fallen just short, you have achieved far more than if you'd played it safe and settled for mediocrity.

But if you do decide to go for it, you need to remember what that great cultural icon of the mid-twentieth century, Elvis Presley, said:

> Ambition is a dream with a V8 engine.
>
> **Elvis Presley**

If you are going to aim high, you have to provide the fire, guts and power that a V8 engine produces if your dreams are going to become a reality.

It's worth keeping both these quotations in mind as you read this chapter.

THEODORE LEVITT ON MAKING YOUR CAREER YOUR BUSINESS

Use this to remind you that you should see your career as you would a business and act accordingly.

Theodore Levitt (1925–2006) was Professor of Economics at The Harvard Business School and played a key role in popularising the term 'globalisation'. He suggested that:

> Your career is literally your business.
>
> **Theodore Levitt**

It would appear that some managers have taken his advice too literally and now spend more time enhancing and maintaining their resumé than in doing what's best for the organisation.

In *The Little Book of Big Management Questions*, I suggested that there are three types of employees:

- **The Workers** are not concerned with promotion and advancement. Their true interests lie outside work, be that amateur dramatics, singing, football or whatever.
- **The Warriors** work hard and are ambitious. They are the future of every business and need to be nurtured.
- **The Wanderers** are only interested in advancing their own career. Every decision they make is based on 'what's best for me'. They are often keen on making changes, as it enhances their CV, but leave before the full (often disastrous) effects of any change made are known. They tend to their image as carefully as any wannabe pop star.

It's the Warriors who need to get the balance right between working hard and presenting the right professional image if they want to avoid being labelled as Workers.

WHAT TO DO

- First impressions count (see Quotation 12), so how you look and present yourself is important:

- Comply with the dress code of your organisation. If it's laid-back and relaxed smart-casual, don't appear in a three-piece pinstripe.
- Ask a friend or partner whether you have any annoying habits and eradicate them. For example, do you: use the word 'like' six times, like, in every, like, sentence or chew your hair, like. OK is another word to avoid adding to every utterance you make. OK?

■ Always appear self-confident but not arrogant – especially when you're feeling terrified. Stand straight, smile and look people in the eye when you speak.

■ Improve your communication skills. People make judgements about you based upon how you speak and write. Keep both your written and spoken English simple, clear and unambiguous and don't join the morons who think that management speak is cool and clever. It isn't! It's dumb and embarrassing.

■ We all have bad days, but aim to produce work at 80 per cent plus of your best as a minimum, day in, day out.

■ Accountants, lawyers and doctors are expected to place their client's interest above their own. As a professional manager, your client is the organisation, so act accordingly and make all your decisions in its best interests.

■ Establish a reputation for honesty and integrity (see Quotation 13) and, once established, protect, enhance and safeguard it.

■ Find a role model in your organisation and fashion your behaviour on theirs. Eventually, you will develop your own unique style and you'll no longer need to ape anyone's behaviour.

■ Keep your professional knowledge up to date. Learn new skills that will increase your expert power (see Quotation 71). Even if you are not thinking about moving, attend at least one interview a year. This will keep you match fit for when you do want to move.

■ Build up your network of business contacts using social media and personal contacts. Become active in professional and trade organisations and use opportunities at work, such as a presentations, to get noticed by senior managers/the board.

QUESTIONS TO ASK

■ In whose interests do I act when I make decisions: my own, my department's/staff's or the organisation's?

■ Do I need a role model? If so, is there anyone I could use in the organisation?

QUOTATION 12 # HENRY FORD ON PURSUING YOUR HEART'S DESIRE

Use this to remind you that if you are doing what you love, it's not work.

Henry Ford (1863–1947) was an American industrialist and founder of the Ford Motor Company. As well as being the champion of mass production, he developed a keen understanding of human nature. He suggested that:

> The whole secret of a successful life is to find out what one's destiny [is], and then do it.
>
> **Henry Ford**

WHAT TO DO

- Identify what you want to do in life and then do it. Sounds simple. But the problem is that many people are unsure of what they want to do and they end up drifting into a job. Usually, people recognise their mistake and dream about what they should be doing. If this is you, try the following. Take a piece of paper and write on the top line what you want to do. Then draw a line down the centre of the page. In the left-hand column, list all the forces that are pushing you to change careers. On the right, list all the forces that are pulling you back and restraining you from making the change.

- Write down everything that comes to mind, from the apparently insignificant to absolutely vital. Draw up this list over several days, recording new issues as they pop into your head.

- Sit down with your completed list and score each factor. There is no limit to the score that you can give to a factor and it's OK to have more than one factor with the same score.

- If one or two forces outscore every other by a country mile, concentrate your attention on these. For example, if the pull of retaining and becoming an actor scores 200 and the fear of giving up financial security for you and your family scores 190, it's probable that all other factors are irrelevant. If that's the case, you have to decide, along with your partner/family, what to do. In talking about it, you may find that they have ideas about how to ameliorate the drop in income that the change would cause. Or you could find that they are so implacably opposed to the change that the real choice you face is losing your family if you change your career. Either way, you will have identified the crux of your dilemma.

■ If there are no major forces operating in either direction, add up the left- and right-hand scores. Let's assume that the holding (stay) forces add up to 110 and the pull (change) forces 130: it would seem obvious that you should go with the pull side. But if you still feel doubtful? You need to revisit the scores. Have you been entirely honest with yourself? Are you overstating the pull factors or have you understated what is really holding you?

■ The final change and stay scores are actually less important than the process you go through. By examining each factor, you will understand much more clearly what is holding and pulling you. This enables you to make a more informed decision than when all the issues were just a jumble in your head.

QUESTIONS TO ASK

■ In an ideal world, what would I like to be doing?

■ Am I doing what I want to do? If not, what is holding me back?

QUOTATION 13 # DALE CARNEGIE ON HOW PEOPLE KNOW YOU

Use this to manage the impact you have on others.

Dale Carnegie (1888–1955), author and businessman, was interested in how people interacted with others and why some seemed to be more effective at influencing people than others. He suggested that:

> There are four ways, and only four ways, in which we have contact with the world. We are evaluated and classified by these four contacts: what we do, how we look, what we say and how we say it.
>
> **Dale Carnegie**

Given that we have only five senses, it is not surprising that we judge people based upon what we see, their actions and appearances, and what we hear, what they say and how they sound. Very occasionally, we might judge someone by how they smell if their body odour or perfume/aftershave overpowers us and renders us senseless!

WHAT TO DO

- In prehistoric times, the ability to judge someone instantly was literally a matter of life or death. If you came across a stranger in the jungle, you had seconds to decide whether they were a friend or someone who'd imbed an axe in your head. Today, we continue to form opinions about people even before they open their mouths. Subconsciously, we're asking ourselves: is this person one of us? Therefore, at work, dress and act appropriately. What that means will vary between organisations and sectors, but you'll quickly pick up on what is required. If it's your first day and you are unsure, smart, stylish and conservative is probably the best bet.

- It's not so long ago that people were judged according to their accents. Thankfully, since the 1990s, this barrier has broken down and we celebrate the diversity of accents. Whatever your accent, it's essential that you are able to speak clear, grammatical English. If people can't hear or understand what you are saying, how can you possibly influence them? Don't mumble, look at the person you're speaking to, speak loud enough to be heard and always speak with confidence (see Quotation 14).

- What you have to say is obviously important. If you are talking nonsense, even if you speak beautifully, you'll still look like a fool. Never speak unless you know what you are talking about. Too many people pass opinions on subjects they know nothing about and end up sounding like dilettantes and amateurs when the experts step in to correct or rebut their arguments. Your credibility is a precious commodity and you need to protect it at all times.

- As for what to do, develop a professional image based on integrity. People respect, listen to and follow those they trust. If, through your actions, you demonstrate that you treat people with respect, equality and fairness and that you will never exploit them or their ideas for your own benefit, you will quickly establish a reputation for integrity.

- Alongside your reputation for integrity, you need to build a reputation for getting things done or doing things differently from other managers. Always underpromise, 'I'll get the job done by Friday' and overdeliver, i.e. finish the job by Thursday (see Quotation 79).

QUESTIONS TO ASK

- Do I know how others perceive me? Have I ever asked friends or colleagues how I come across to other people?

- Am I too quick to jump to conclusions about people based on how they look or sound?

QUOTATION 14 HENRY FORD ON SELF-CONFIDENCE AND SELF-DOUBT (TOP TEN ENTRY)

Use this to help you build self-confidence and destroy self-doubt.

In the following quotation, Henry Ford (1863–1947) provides the reason why some people succeed and so many fail and it has nothing to do with accidents of birth, intelligence or opportunities. It's all down to confidence.

> The man who thinks he can and the one who thinks he can't are both right. Which one are you?
>
> **Henry Ford**

Only psychopaths, politicians and other lunatics exhibit total self-confidence. The rest of us have self-doubts. It's what makes us reasonable, cautious people. However, you should never allow your self-doubts to stop you from trying to do something that you desperately want to do. If you try something, you may fail because of circumstances beyond your control. That's the chance you take. But if you don't try, you are doomed to failure and regret.

WHAT TO DO

- As a philosophy to live by, and as a way of increasing your self-confidence in all walks of life, follow Eleanor Roosevelt's advice and 'Do one thing every day that scares you.' It doesn't have to be big, it may be asking a question in a public meeting or going up to the best-looking man or woman in the room and asking them to dance. Pushing the boundaries in little things will help you to face your fears when it comes to more significant events.

- Generally, we lack self-confidence when faced with a new task or situation. Once you've completed the task or been through the situation, the nerves disappear. So force yourself to accept the challenge of the new. Volunteer for what scares you. Do this consistently and pretty soon you'll find that your confidence in tackling new tasks and situations will grow exponentially. You may still have the odd few butterflies in the stomach but they won't stop you from doing what you want to do. Indeed, you'll need them and the adrenalin they produce to do your best work.

- Remember, if you appear to lack faith in your own abilities or the recommendations you make, why should your boss, colleagues or staff trust your judgement?

- Exhibit self-confidence at all times – especially when you're terrified. How you feel is immaterial. It's how you are perceived by your bosses, staff, colleagues, competitors, business partners, bankers, etc. that is all-important. Confide your worries to friends and family but never to work colleagues. Act confidently until you become confident.

- Finally, use positive self-talk and visualisation to improve your own self-confidence/belief and celebrate your own success in whatever way you find most rewarding – because, after all, you're worth it (I've been watching too much Living TV).

QUESTIONS TO ASK

- On a scale of 1 to 10, where 10 is very confident, how confident am I generally at work, in social situations and in formal situations? If my score is less than 7 across the board, what am I going to do to improve it?

- Why do I lack self-confidence? Is it because of something said or done to me in childhood? If so, why do I allow such ancient events to affect me today?

QUOTATION 15 MOLLY SARGENT ON INVESTING IN YOUR GREATEST ASSET – YOURSELF

Use this to remind you of the need to continue learning and developing as a person and manager.

Molly Sargent, management consultant and founder of ProImpress, is interested in organisational and personal development. Therefore, it's not surprising that she is concerned with asking managers, at all levels, how much they spend on personal development. But she has a unique way of phrasing the question:

> Have you invested as much this year in your career as your car?
>
> **Molly Sargent**

Well – did you?

My future   My car

WHAT TO DO

- Our greatest asset is ourselves, but assets will become dilapidated unless they are constantly maintained and improved. For us, maintenance requires us to stay abreast of the latest changes in our professional field while improvement requires that we learn new skills. To do this properly, you need to undertake an annual training needs analysis.
- A training needs analysis involves:
  - listing the skills and abilities that you have and the level at which you can deploy them, e.g. beginner, intermediate and expert level;
  - listing the skills that you require to continue doing your job to a high level;

- comparing the two lists and identifying any shortfalls in skills required or level;
- drawing up a plan of action to eliminate any shortfalls.

■ While you can undertake your own training needs analysis, it is better to get an expert to help you. They will be able to probe and challenge your ideas and suggest ways to move forward. Use someone from your training department or a friend who works in human resources to help you.

■ The solutions to your problem may involve doing a bit of reading, learning from an expert on how they do a particular job, shadowing a member of staff or undertaking a training session at the offices/ factory of a supplier. This simple low-cost approach may improve your productivity considerably as it's likely that you'll find you are using only a small percentage of the facilities available on the new computer system/machine. Don't believe me? What percentage of Excel, PowerPoint or Word can you/your staff use?

■ More formal arrangement might require going on a short course or undertaking a further qualification.

■ Once you've identified what is required, you must be willing to invest the time and money required to undertake the training. Yes, by all means try and get your organisation to pay some or all of the fees. But if they say no, **pay for it yourself!** After all, it's you who will gain the greatest benefit from the training.

■ Look to enhance your skills in an area where your organisation has little or no expertise. For example, accountants might look to obtain a qualification in cyber security. This will give you a competitive advantage when seeking promotion or applying for jobs and increase your expert power (see Quotation 71).

■ Every year, identify a sum of money that you will set aside for your own professional development and then **spend it**.

QUESTIONS TO ASK

■ How many hours did I spend on professional development last year?
■ How much did I spend on my professional development last year?

QUOTATION 16 # ANDREW CARNEGIE ON WHY YOU CAN'T DO IT ALL YOURSELF

Use this to remind you that you must delegate work if you are to be successful.

Andrew Carnegie (1835–1919), the Scottish American industrialist and philanthropist, made his fortune in steel and, while he had the confidence to build an immense organisation, he had the humility to say:

> No person will make a great business who wants to do it all himself or get all the credit.
>
> **Andrew Carnegie**

WHAT TO DO

- Follow the advice given by Warren Buffet about appointing good staff in the first place (see Quotation 25). Once you've appointed good people, get out of their way and let them do their job (see Quotation 27).

- Assess how good you are at delegating work. List the work that you have delegated in the last month. Analyse the jobs under simple, medium and complex tasks. If you delegate only simple tasks, your failure to challenge staff with more interesting and rewarding work may demotivate them (see Quotation 45).

- If you fail to delegate because you fear either losing control or being criticised for dumping work on staff, use Ken Blanchard's and Paul Hersey's situational leadership theory as a model for delegation. They suggest that each time you delegate a new piece of work to someone, you have to identify the level of direction and support the person requires. Direction relates to the level of instruction you need to provide on how to do the actual job. Support relates to the amount of reassurance, encouragement and hand-holding you need to provide as the person finds their feet. By combining the level of direction and support, four possible delegation strategies arise:

Approach to delegation	Description of behaviour
Coaching	High direction and high support is provided where the person lacks knowledge of how to do the job and has little self-confidence/belief.
Directing	The directing mode is used when high direction and low support is provided to those who are self-confident but lack experience of the work.
Supporting	High support and low direction is provided to those who are experienced enough to do the work but worry about taking on new work.
Delegating	A low support and low direction approach is used with those who have high levels of technical skills and are self-confident and assured.

- Select the most suitable person for the job. Brief them on what needs to be done and get a feel for how they are feeling. Ask questions such as, 'Can you explain to me what you are going to do first?' 'Is there anything that worries you about what I've asked you to do?'

- Based on your discussion, select the model of delegation you think is most appropriate.

- Agree a deadline for the completion of the work and specify the criteria that the finished work has to meet.

- If the job is going to take several weeks, book an early review meeting to discuss progress. Based on that meeting, decide whether further meetings are required.

- Emphasise that if the person runs into problems, they can see you immediately.

- Remember, people don't move through the four approaches outlined above in any recognisable sequence. Every time you give a person a new job/task, you have to identify which approach to use with them.

QUESTIONS TO ASK

- How often do I delegate work?
- How much time do I spend explaining what's required when I delegate work?

QUOTATION 17 # THOMAS EDISON ON WHY PERSISTENCE NOT INSPIRATION LEADS TO SUCCESS

Use this to motivate yourself when everything is going against you.

Thomas Edison (1847–1931), American inventor and founder of General Electric Corporation, famously failed to make a working electric light bulb 999 times, or so the myth goes, but was successful on his 1,000th attempt. He probably invented that story to show what a vital part persistence plays in any final success.

> Many of life's failures are people who did not realise how close they were to success when they gave up.
>
> **Thomas Edison**

Very often people overcome the huge initial problems they face only to give up halfway through the project. This is because initial enthusiasm has waned, finishing the project seems a long way off and everything you've managed to do to date appears to be total rubbish. I know the feeling; I've been there with every project I've ever managed or book I've written. It's natural to feel that way. So, take a deep breath and press on.

WHAT TO DO

■ Accept that in the middle of every complex undertaking it is almost certainly going to look like a failure. You're tired. Your team are tired. The initial enthusiasm with which you started the project has dwindled. The end is nowhere in sight. It's then that you must remember what Winston Churchill said, 'Keep buggering on.'

■ Plan for the inevitable attacks that will occur during the desolate middle of your project. This is when you and the project are at your most vulnerable. Gerard Egan in his Shadow Side theory argues that managers must manage different stakeholders within an organisation if they are to be successful. He categorises the stakeholders into nine categories (see *The Little Book of Big Management Theories* for a full description). Two categories are particularly relevant to this situation, namely Opponents and Adversaries. Opponents are those who oppose the project but have nothing against you personally, while Adversaries oppose both you and your project. They will wait until you and the project are at your weakest point that mid-point when nothing concrete has been achieved, but a lot of time, effort and money has been invested in the project, and then they will strike.

- You must expect such an attack and be prepared to deal with it by identifying and getting onside your supporters. According to Egan, these include Partners who support the project and Allies, who, if encouraged enough, will support you.

- Identify the likely focus of any attacks, e.g. it's too expensive, it's not going to work, there are better alternatives, and have a well-argued rebuttal for each claim. Don't rely on emotion. Rely on facts and figures.

- Remember, as the agenda for change rolls out, it will affect more people. In focusing on the Opponents and Adversaries, don't lose sight of the importance of consolidating your Partners and Allies.

- Recognise that this theory is concerned with organisational politics (see Quotations 61 and 73) and that, without some understanding of organisational politics, you'll be out-manoeuvred by those who play the game better.

QUESTIONS TO ASK

- Who can I rely on when the going gets tough? Do I know who will attack me and do I have a response strategy?
- How well prepared am I for dealing with organisational politics? Do I need to learn more?

BILL WATKINS ON WHY YOU SHOULD NEVER ASK MANAGEMENT FOR THEIR OPINION

Use this to remind you that people who provide answers go further and get more done than those who ask questions.

Bill Watkins (b. 1953), an American business executive and former CEO of Seagate Technology, speaking to *Fortune Magazine* in November 2006, put on record a truism that every manager should know and live by:

> You never ask board members what they think. You tell them what you are going to do.
>
> **Bill Watkins**

What Bill Watkins says applies to any manager or group that you are reporting to. If you ask people what they think, they will feel obliged to come up with something, no matter how daft, and then you will have to evaluate it and report back, explaining (nicely) why it's the worst idea since the Red Socks sold Babe Ruth to the New York Yankees.

WHAT TO DO

- Before you present a written or verbal report to your manager/board, make sure that you have done your homework and that you have considered and evaluated all the main issues and possible courses of action. Do this and you will know more about the subject under consideration than anyone else in the room.

- As the de facto expert on the issues under discussion, you are in the best position to make an informed recommendation on how to proceed. If you don't do this, then your manager/board will discuss the issues from their less well-informed positions and you'll end up having to evaluate or, worse, implement one of the half-baked solutions they come up with. Yes, I accept that, occasionally, they will come up with a better solution – but not very often in my experience or that of Bill Watkins.

- Structure your verbal or written report in a logical order that leads the person through the issues step by step. As you proceed, very briefly, discuss those solutions that you have considered and rejected. This will stop people raising them later.

- Don't spring any surprises on your manager/board. From the introduction onwards, your report should be building towards your final recommendation, funnelling the person's thinking in one direction only. Do this right and, when you finally make your recommendation, it will appear, to all present, the only possible way to proceed.

- Writing reports/making a pitch are skills and, like any other, can be learned and improved with practice (see *The Little Book of Big Management Questions* for advice on writing and presentations).

- There are definitely brownie points to be earned by presenting solutions rather than questions or requests for their views. Make good, clear, firm recommendations and people will see you as a confident, professional problem solver who knows how to get things done. These are the attributes you need to be known for if you are to progress to the very top.

QUESTIONS TO ASK

- Do I ask for people's views or present solutions when reporting issues to my boss/board?
- Would I benefit from getting some professional advice about how to make my written and personal presentations more effective?

QUOTATION 19

ANDREW CARNEGIE ON INVESTING 100 PER CENT OF YOUR ENERGY IN YOUR CAREER

Use this to remind you that 75 per cent effort isn't enough if you want to excel.

Andrew Carnegie (1835–1919), one of the greatest nineteenth-century century American industrialists, did not rise from the poverty of a one-room weaver's cottage in Dunfermline to international renown by investing only part of his energy in his work.

> The average person puts about 25 per cent of his [sic] energy into his work. The world takes its hat off to those who put more than 50 per cent of their capacity, and stands on its head for those few and far between souls who devote 100 per cent.
>
> **Andrew Carnegie**

Carnegie would have been bewildered by the present-day discussion on work–life balance. For him work was his life. The same is true of those who have excelled in the arts, humanities and sciences. There are very few, if any, who coasted to greatness.

WHAT TO DO

- You have to decide how much time and effort you wish to invest in your career and what sacrifices you are willing to make to achieve your dreams. Unless you are willing to 'go full in', it's unlikely that you'll reach the very top.
- No matter what your age or present position, if you want to stand out from the crowd, you need to think strategically about your career (see Section 2).
- Start by setting your ultimate objective. Provide as much detail of your objective as possible and what it will feel like to achieve it. This 'vision' will help you stay the course when things become difficult – and they will.
- Establish a series of targets that will move you towards achievement of your objective. Break these down into a series of short- (less than

one year), medium- (two to five years) and long-term (six to ten year) targets. Note that targets set more than a year in advance are little more than a pious wish. Therefore, update your plans on a rolling basis to take account of new information and your success and failures.

■ Ensure that all your targets are SMART i.e..

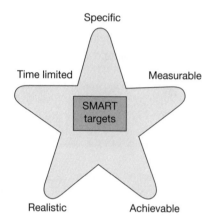

■ You've now got some idea of what you want to achieve and what you need to do to reach your objective. Now is the time to ask yourself whether you are willing to pay the price required to be successful. Your pursuit of success means sacrifice. Look at the other activities in your life and the time you spend on them. These include family, socialising, sleep, hobbies, holidays, etc. Which are you willing to give up or reduce to realise your ambitions? It's a tough question but you need to ask and answer it.

■ Unless you are in a job that has little or no need for input from others, such as writing, you will be able to achieve your objectives only through the work of others. Therefore, you must learn to delegate if you wish to increase your productivity (see Quotations 16 and 27).

QUESTIONS TO ASK

■ How much additional time do I need to devote to work in order to achieve my objectives? Where can I find that time? (See Quotation 20).

■ If I'm not willing to reduce the time I spend on non-work related activities, do I need to review my objectives or can I still achieve them by working smarter (delegate more)?

QUOTATION 20

THOMAS EDISON ON SAVING TIME

Use this to help you manage your time and achieve your objectives.

Thomas Edison (1847–1931) patented over 1,000 inventions in his lifetime. Even though many of these were actually developed by his workers, he was the driving creative force behind them. There is no way he could have achieved so much in his 84 years if he'd wasted time.

> One cannot buy, rent or hire more time. The supply of time is totally inelastic. No matter how high the demand, the supply will not go up.
>
> **Thomas Edison**

One way to get ahead is to work when you're supposed to, play when you're supposed to and not mix the two.

WHAT TO DO

- Learn to say no. Don't allow people to steal your time. Don't allow colleagues to swallow up hours each week talking about everything from their partners to what was on TV the night before, or doing jobs that your staff have messed up. Learn to say no in all its forms and, if necessary, go on an assertiveness course.

- Keep a detailed record of what you do over a week – and, yes, you should include your chats about the football and the latest bit of juicy gossip. You'll be amazed at the rubbish you allow yourself to be dragged into.

- Use The Eisenhower Time Management Grid to help you free up time that you can spend on the vital stuff that will help you achieve your targets and objectives. Start by analysing each task that crosses your desk, placing it into one of the following categories and follow the advice for each.

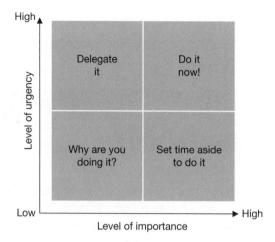

- **Do it now!:** This includes demands from your boss and the need to meet urgent deadlines.
- **Set time aside to do it:** These are jobs that, if done now will save you time in the future by resolving ongoing problems at source. Unfortunately, they usually take a backseat to the urgent stuff. Use the time saved by not getting involved in the following two categories of work to deal with them.
- **Why are you doing it?** These are tasks that you should not be doing and should be avoided by you and your team. Bin or delegate it.
- **Delegate it:** There are other people's crises that they try to make yours. If you want to help, delegate it.
- If you have the self-discipline and assertiveness required, Eisenhower's model can save you time which you can then invest in projects that will increase your productivity and get you noticed.
- Eisenhower's model deals with the clock, about the things you have to do in the short term. You also need to think about the calendar. The calendar contains those long-term jobs, targets and objectives that you will be judged on at some time in the future. Never lose track of these (see Quotation 19).

QUESTIONS TO ASK

- How good am I at prioritising my work? Am I a slave to the urgent?
- When was the last time that I analysed what I do over a week?

CONCLUSION

The Top Ten entry from this section is Ford's quotation on self-confidence:

> The man who thinks he can and the one who thinks he can't are both right. Which one are you?
>
> **Henry Ford**

For me this was an easy choice to make. Self-confidence is the bedrock of success. Without self-confidence you will never be successful, no matter how well-qualified, intelligent or hard-working you are. Why am I so certain? To succeed, you need other people to believe in you, including your staff, colleagues and bosses. If you lack self-confidence, it will be taken as a sign of weakness and that you lack belief in your own abilities. In that situation, people will rightly ask themselves, 'If s/he doesn't believe in themselves, why should I?'

I suspect that we are all born with a hefty supply of self-confidence. Unfortunately, as we grow and develop, life, disappointments and the words and actions of others knock it out of us. We need to replenish it, guard it and celebrate it.

Start today and follow the advice in Quotation 14; do something every day that scares you. The more you fear doing something, the quicker you should run towards it. By embracing what really frightens/intimidates you, your self-confidence will grow by leaps and bounds and infect all areas of your life.

ONE LESSON TO TAKE AWAY

If you currently lack confidence in certain situations, fake it. Act with confidence, even if the butterflies in your stomach are playing the *1812 Overture* and using real cannons. Keep acting for a while and pretty soon the act will give way to genuine confidence.

SECTION 3

MANAGING PEOPLE AND TEAMS

INTRODUCTION

There are a wide range of skills associated with the practice of management. In this section I've tried to identify the key knowledge and understanding that you require to be a successful manager. It has been difficult to choose the final 12 from the many hundreds that I read, but in the end I selected those that I thought would be most useful to a busy manager. The quotations are arranged into five groups. Quotations:

- 21 to 23 deal with the nature of management and the role of the manager.
- 24 and 25 are about when you should recruit staff and what you need to look for.
- 26 and 27 offer advice on managing people.
- 28 to 30 consider how to monitor performance.
- 31 and 32 explain why staff training and development are essential if you and your organisation are to be successful.

One quality that is seldom mentioned in management books specifically is common sense. Perhaps writers think it's too obvious to merit a mention. However, it's worth remembering what Gerald B. Blair said:

> The first step to becoming a really great manager is [to possess] simple common sense, but common sense is not very common.
>
> **Gerald B. Blair**

Anyone can dream up impractical solutions to a problem. It's the constraints you work under that often make solving a problem difficult. In these circumstances you need to come forward with practical solutions. That's where a bit of common sense comes in. Usually, the common-sense solution is the simplest one on offer. As you read this section you'll see that simplicity underpins many of the ideas discussed.

QUOTATION 21 # CHARLES HANDY ON WHAT MANAGEMENT SHOULD BE ABOUT

Use this to realise that management is infinitely complex and should be enjoyable, even when it's hard.

Charles Handy (b. 1932) is an academic, business executive and probably the most respected British writer on management and leadership.

He was echoing the views of Robert Townsend (see Quotations 24 and 49) when he said:

> Management is more fun, more creative, more personal, more political and more intuitive than any text book.
>
> **Charles Handy**

Too often, management is treated with a certain pious reverence. Yes, management is serious but how you carry out that function doesn't have to be without a sense of creativity, fun and humour.

WHAT TO DO

- Fun has a bad name in management. If you're having fun, you can't be serious. What rubbish. Morecombe and Wise, the Marx Brothers, Will Smith and Clint Eastwood are or were supreme professionals in their own field and worked amazingly hard at their art but they have/had fun doing it. In this context, fun means enjoying what you do and having the time to share that enjoyment with the people around you. Do this and your sense of enjoyment will rub off on other people and improve the atmosphere and therefore the morale and motivation of your staff.

- Management is not a natural science. There are no universal rules that apply to it. Management is always time, place, person and situation dependent. To deal with this you have to be constantly creative. You have past experience, knowledge of management theories and models, and some understanding of the people you are dealing with. This is your palate of colours from which you can either paint a masterpiece or a dreadful mess. Management is an art

and the more you practise the better you'll become. Don't be afraid
to make mistakes; experiment with different approaches and always
remain flexible in your thinking.

- Management involves dealing with people. The more you know about
  them, their attitude to work and life, their views and opinions, their
  dreams and ambitions, the better able you will be to predict their
  reaction in any given situation and how best to handle them. To learn
  about people, keep your mouth shut and your ears open. Remember,
  you have two ears and one mouth: use them in that proportion.

- In any organisation, even a family, there is an element of political
  manoeuvring. In a few, dysfunctional organisations, people spend
  more time playing politics than doing their job. It's entirely up to you
  whether you want to play the political game or not. However, you
  should know enough to be able to defend yourself from political
  attack, so read Quotations 61 and 73.

- You know more about your organisation than you are capable of
  communicating to any other person. This tacit knowledge is held in
  your subconscious mind. When this knowledge is used, it's often
  called intuition or gut instinct. Never ignore your gut instinct. If your
  gut is telling you one thing and the numbers another, recheck the
  numbers.

QUESTIONS TO ASK

- Do I have fun at work? If not, is it because I'm in the wrong job, trade
  or profession?

- Am I over-reliant on hard data when managing staff and/or making
  decisions? Do I need to pay more attention to the soft, intuitive data?

PETER DRUCKER AND THE MANAGER'S JOB IN 13 WORDS

Use this as a guide to the essential elements of management.

Peter Drucker (1909–2005) was an Austrian-born American. He was an academic, management consultant and writer and has been credited with laying the foundation for the academic discipline that we now call management studies. He suggested that managers have five primary functions. They should:

> Set objectives, organise resources, motivate staff, monitor performance and develop people including themselves.
>
> **Peter Drucker**

WHAT TO DO

- Use the objectives that have been set for you and your team by management as your starting point.
- Working with your staff, break the objectives down into a series of SMART targets (see Quotation 19), achievement of which will mean that the objective has been met.
- Allocate responsibility for achievement of the target to a named individual. Set 80 per cent of the targets at a level that is relatively easy to achieve. This will turn people on to success and motivate them to meet the more challenging targets.
- Monitor progress against target and take corrective action when required (see Quotation 29).
- Constantly monitor the physical and staffing resources that you need to achieve your targets and take action to remedy any shortfalls before they become a problem.
- Motivate and communicate with your staff by sharing information and listening to what they have to say. In addition, recognise what Herzberg says about staff motivation (see Quotation 45) and ensure that every job has enough content to satisfy the person's need for interesting work that they can feel proud of doing.

- If your career is your business (see Quotation 11), you are the greatest asset it has, invest time and energy in developing both your technical and managerial skills. Develop expertise in an area that would be of value to your organisation and its competitors, e.g. 3D printing. Keep yourself match fit by attending interviews regularly.
- If you are ever asked to define management or the role of managers, trot out Drucker's definition above as if it were your own.
- Your staff are your second greatest asset, so develop, train and support them.

QUESTIONS TO ASK

- Am I a manager or an administrator, i.e. do I spend my day working at my desk, or helping others to do their work?
- Who is the best manager in the organisation? What can I learn from them?

PETER DRUCKER ON LEARNING TO WORK WITH WHAT YOU'VE GOT

Use this to remind you that you will never have the perfect team or system.

The godfather of management science, Peter Drucker (1919–2005) was a very practical man. He didn't dream up theories or ideas based on what he thought should happen or what could happen in business. His ideas were based on what did happen in business.

As a football fan, I've lost count of the times that a manager has subtly blamed his squad of players for the team's poor performance. Phrases such as 'We need two or three new players in the next transfer window' are code for 'Don't blame me for the last six defeats, I didn't sign these donkeys.'

But Drucker knew it was a manager's job to manage with the resources that s/he had available to them:

> The task is to manage what there is and work to create what could or should be.
>
> **Peter Drucker**

WHAT TO DO

- If you are short of the tools, machines, systems and materials to do your job, you must renegotiate your targets and objectives or else find a way to beg, borrow or steal what you require. But really you should never have agreed to the targets and objectives in the first place.
- More likely, your problems will be with staff and the skills they do and don't have. Start by examining the targets and objectives that you and your staff have been set.
- Identify the skills required to achieve the targets and objectives to a good standard.
- Analyse the skills that your staff currently possess.
- Compare the skills sets of your staff with the skills required to achieve your objectives and identify any shortfalls.

- Consider to what extent formal or informal training might eliminate or reduce some of the shortfalls and arrange any training that is required. Obviously, training will have to be delivered quickly and be capable of having a near instantaneous effect. We're not talking about long training programmes or professional courses here. You'll be looking at short-term sessions delivered in-house, perhaps by you or other staff, which will plug skill gaps in the short term or by the suppliers of systems and machines that you have recently purchased.

- Redistribute work in order to play to the strengths of individual members of staff.

- Assuming that you can't appoint a new member of staff, check whether anyone has a member of staff that they are willing to lend to you in the short term. But beware of managers offloading their greatest unresolved problem.

- As people leave, use the 'skills required analysis' that you completed as the basis for drawing up a new job description and/or person specification. With 20 per cent staff turnover now fairly normal, you should be able to resolve most, if not all, your problems within two or three years.

QUESTIONS TO ASK

- When did I last undertake an analysis of the skills required by my staff and compare that to the skills they have?

- When did I last reorganise/redistribute work responsibilities within the team in order to play to people's strengths?

ROBERT TOWNSEND ON HOW TO KEEP THE ORGANISATION LEAN, FIT AND VITAL

Use this to help you decide when to expand the workforce.

Robert Townsend (1920–98) was an American businessman who is best known for turning Avis Rent a Car into the giant company it is today and for his number-one bestseller *Up the Organisation*, a book which, I believe, should be on every management course reading list in the world.

His often humorous asides, suggestions and exaggerations usually contain within them an essential truth, e.g.:

> To keep an organisation young and fit, don't hire anyone until everyone is so overworked they'll be glad to see the newcomer and won't mind where they sit.
>
> **Robert Townsend**

Townsend is not suggesting that you work people into the ground. However, he recognises that very often an organisation will create a post almost as soon as the workload starts to increase and there is insufficient work to keep the newcomer occupied, which can cause friction with other staff.

WHAT TO DO

- Recognise that people like to be busy at work and that a certain amount of pressure is good for both staff morale and productivity. When a team is busy they often pull together. A shared sense of purpose and pride in working hard unites and motivates them. So don't jump in with new staff too soon.
- Look for the signs that people are genuinely overworked rather than just busy. Such signs include: increased sickness and staff turnover, missed deadlines, short tempers and arguments between staff members and staff and managers.
- The trick is to react to the increased workload just before the problems listed above occur. This is not easy. It's the type of

judgement call that relies on your knowledge of the staff and business conditions. Is it just a temporary increase in work or is it here to stay? If a hard-working member of staff who seldom complains is wilting and moaning about workloads, you need to respond to what is happening. Rely on your tacit knowledge to make the call.

- Tacit knowledge, or what Professor John Adair calls deep knowledge, resides in your subconscious but informs your thinking and actions on a daily basis without you being aware of it. This unconscious knowledge is the sum total of all you know about your job, the organisation and the people who work in it. The more information you can collect, the more useful this knowledge will be to you. Therefore, use meetings, management by walking about, conversations at the coffee machine or over lunch and every other interaction you have with staff, customers, suppliers and investors to add to your store of knowledge.

- Record briefly any interesting comments, events, trends, problems, opportunities, threats or juicy gossip in your learning journal (see How to get the most out of this book).

- All of the above information will compost down in your subconscious and form linkages and connections in your brain which will enrich your tacit knowledge. When faced with a problem, this knowledge will resurface and provide you with an answer.

QUESTIONS TO ASK

- When was the last time I checked that everyone in my team was fully employed?
- Is there anyone in my team who is overworked? Do I need to redistribute work?

QUOTATION 25

WARREN BUFFET ON WHY INTEGRITY TRUMPS INTELLIGENCE AND ENERGY WHEN APPOINTING PEOPLE (TOP TEN ENTRY)

Use this to remind you of the key characteristics you should be looking for when you appoint or promote staff.

Warren Buffet (b. 1930), the world's leading investment manager, likes to keep things simple: e.g. his investment strategy is to buy good stocks and hold them for a long time. He has applied the same simplicity to the appointment of staff and suggests that there are three things you should look for when recruiting people:

> Somebody once said that in looking for people to hire, you look for three qualities: integrity, intelligence and energy. And if they don't have the first, the other two will kill you. You think about it; it's true. If you hire somebody without integrity, you really [do] want them to be dumb and lazy.
>
> **Warren Buffet**

Integrity is the key factor for Buffet. If a person lacks integrity, they are a danger to the organisation. Indeed, much of the 2008 financial meltdown can be blamed on a lack of integrity among highly intelligent and well-motivated bankers.

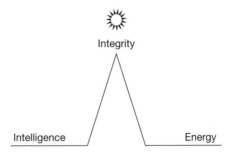

WHAT TO DO

- Whenever possible, promote from within. Such a policy creates staff loyalty and you are less likely to appoint a dud because you (should) know the person's strengths and weaknesses. Only if you need new blood or a skill set not found in your organisation should you consider going outside.

- At the interview concentrate on identifying which applicant/s demonstrate integrity, intelligence and energy. If you can spot those, then any shortfalls in skills can be taught.

- Integrity/character is the hardest trait to confirm. Look at how the person presents themselves. Are they confident without being arrogant? Do they recognise that they don't have all the answers? Do they take pride in their work and achievements? If they do, they won't want to let themselves and, by implication, you down. Do they talk about what they and their team have achieved or is it all about them? Ask them about any ethical dilemma that they faced in the past and how they dealt with it. The problem doesn't have to be work-related. If they can't think of an example, it's very likely that they have few, if any, guiding principles.

- Intelligence is fairly easy to identify. Obviously, start by looking at the person's educational attainments. However, their interaction with you or the interview panel will tell you more than any certificate. Do their answers show a level of analysis? Do they try to contextualise their responses in terms of your organisation? Can they see the bigger picture and how their work will fit into the whole? Are they inquisitive and interested in your operation? Do they possess common sense or are their ideas unworkable in the real world?

- Energy and enthusiasm is easy to spot. Simply ask yourself, 'Do I feel energised speaking to this person?' If the answer is 'yes', then other people are likely to be similarly enthused by the applicant.

QUESTIONS TO ASK

- What's the first thing I look for when appointing or promoting people?
- How successful has my current approach to recruitment and promotion been?

MARCUS BUCKINGHAM ON MANAGERS AND THE GOLDEN RULE

Use this as the basis of your relationship with staff and colleagues.

The Golden Rule suggests that you should treat people as you would like to be treated. Marcus Buckingham (b. 1966), management writer, argues that to be effective, managers should not always treat staff as they would like to be treated. He suggests that:

> The best managers break the Golden Rule every day [as the rule] presupposes that everyone breathes the same psychological oxygen as you [the manager]. For example, if you are competitive, everyone must be similarly competitive. If you like to be praised in public, everyone else must, too.
>
> **Marcus Buckingham**

The fact that people differ is obviously true. Not everyone will share their manager's views and attitudes about work. Nor should they. We all have our own priorities, hopes and dreams and these may have very little to do with our work. But the Golden Rule is not concerned with the tactical issues outlined by Buckingham. It deals with the strategic relationship that should exist between all people, a relationship based on mutual respect and that I think most people want but few ever find at work, whatever their level in the organisation.

WHAT TO DO

- As suggested by Immanuel Kant, you should always remember that individuals are ends in themselves. Do not use them as a means of achieving your ends, especially if they are harmed in the process.
- Accept that every person deserves a level of unconditional respect, simply because they are a human being. You may not like them. You may not agree with them, but they are fellow human beings and should be treated as such.
- When considering people for promotion or appointment, the only acceptable form of discrimination is who's best qualified/suited for the job.

- Don't exploit staff, especially those who are willing to work ridiculous hours to get the job done without extra pay. Either reallocate some of their work or ensure that their pay/status reflects their efforts.
- Never steal ideas from staff and claim them as your own.
- Ensure that people's achievements are recognised in an appropriate way.
- Don't indulge in mushroom management (keeping staff in the dark and regularly shovelling manure on them). Unless information is genuinely sensitive, keep staff informed of any and all events that affect them.
- Don't treat staff as idiots. They may not be as smart or well-educated as you, but they can see through management bullshit, shams and contrived and manipulative presentations and speeches from a thousand metres.
- Deal with people as individuals who have a life outside of work. Learn about their interests and passions, partner and children and what their hopes and ambitions are.
- Be willing to listen to staff's ideas, concerns and worries, and take action if appropriate. Often, staff recognise that you can do nothing about the issue they have raised with you. They just want to express their feeling and have you acknowledge how they feel.
- If you treat people as intelligent adults, they will respond accordingly.

QUESTIONS TO ASK

- How much do I know about the people who work for me?
- Do I view staff as people or just another resource which I have to get the most out of?

THEODORE ROOSEVELT ON WHY YOU SHOULD NOT MICRO-MANAGE STAFF

Use this as a reminder to let your staff get on with their job.

Theodore Roosevelt (1858–1919) was the 26th President of the United States of America. He was also a respected writer and is listed by many as one of the three smartest presidents to occupy the White house (the other two are Abraham Lincoln and John F. Kennedy).

As the driving force behind the Progressive Movement in the Republican Party, he promoted intense social and political change in American society during his presidency. He knew that he could not bring about the changes required alone, and lived by the maxim:

> The best executive is the one who has sense enough to pick good men [sic] to do what needs to be done and the self-restraint to keep from meddling while they do it.
>
> **Theodore Roosevelt**

It's important to recognise that this quotation isn't about delegation; it's about granting staff freedom from interference and the discretion they need to do their job well.

WHAT TO DO

- Invest time and energy in appointing the right people, especially to key posts. A key post can be the supervisor's job on the assembly line or chief accountant. The point is that if you select the wrong person for either job, you're going to have problems (see Quotation 25).
- Staff at all levels are motivated by interesting work, achievement, recognition and responsibility (see Quotation 45). If you are looking over a person's shoulder all the time, they will assume that you don't trust them to do a good job. This will undermine their self-confidence, which will leach into their work, and their performance levels will drop. So resist the temptation to interfere. Instead, establish a culture of trust and support with your staff. To do this:

- Discuss with each person their job. Clarify their responsibilities and clearly define their area of discretion.
- Maintain a genuine open door policy. If a person runs into a problem, encourage them to talk to you, but don't hold the discussion with one eye on the clock as many managers do. Staff know when they are been given 'the bum's rush' and will think twice about approaching you again.
- Insist on regular reports on targets and objectives. But avoid these becoming a rollicking session and remember public hangings ended in Britain in 1868. The discussion should be about solutions, not recriminations.
- Insist on being told bad news as soon as it arises and don't shoot the messenger.
- Celebrate publicly people's successes. This can range from a public acknowledgement of a job well done to a promotion.
- Never blame anyone for an honest mistake. Everyone makes mistakes. It's what they learn from them that matters. If the error is due to carelessness, negligence or plain old-fashioned stupidity, you should take action to ensure it doesn't reoccur.

■ Flowers grow when you feed and water them, not when you regularly pull them out of the ground and inspect the roots to see how things are going. The same is true of staff. The more freedom of action a person has, the better able they are to deal with challenges that arise.

QUESTIONS TO ASK

■ How much do I trust my staff?

■ How often does my monitoring of staff work become interference?

QUOTATION 28 # DEE HOCK ON WHY YOU SHOULD KEEP IT SIMPLE, STUPID (KISS)

Use this to avoid the dangers of relying on over-complex, stultifying systems.

Dee Hock (b. 1929) is the founder and former CEO of the Visa Credit Card Association. He believes that:

> Simple, clear purpose and principles give rise to complex and intelligent behaviour. Complex rules and regulations give rise to simple and stupid behaviour.
>
> **Dee Hock**

How an organisation works and behaves is driven by the systems, rules and procedures that it has. Unfortunately, systems and procedures are seldom designed by the people who use them. Yes, system analysts or consultants will talk to staff about what is required. Unfortunately, much of the information that staff have about their job is tacit knowledge (see Quotation 24). This is knowledge that everyone has but can't be accessed on demand as it resides in a person's subconscious. Such information can't be systemised or fully captured in a procedure document and, if the implemented system does not allow enough wriggle room for staff to exercise their discretion when required, problems will arise.

WHAT TO DO

- How many times have you heard someone say, 'The system won't let me do that.' When *'that'* is obviously the right thing to do. People are flexible, systems and rules seldom are. Don't try to over-systemise everything and always allow for intelligent humans, with proper controls in place, to override the system when it's sensible to do so. For example, many years ago I found a small sliver of wood in a cake I bought from a well-known supermarket. I complained and the Supervisor, without reference to anyone, suggested that I select a Christmas cake in compensation. I was very satisfied with the outcome. Recently, I had a similar experience with the same store. This time it was part of a button and I was required to fill in a form. I then waited approximately four weeks for the complaint to be considered and resolved in accordance with the company's customer care procedures. I was not impressed.

■ Provide people with a clear definition of the organisation's purpose and list the principles that it will always seek to uphold. Even in a very large organisation you should be able to summarise these on one side of A4 paper. **If you can't, your organisation is probably confusing its staff**.

■ Make it clear that these principles override any subsequent policy or procedure that contradicts them and, most importantly, that staff will never be disciplined for following the organisation's purpose and/or principles in good faith.

■ If you've employed good people (see Quotation 25) who understand the purpose and ethos of the organisation, they can be trusted to exercise discretion according to those guidelines when required. They will certainly be more sensitive to the situation than any system that was designed by someone who had no personal experience of the work your staff do.

QUESTIONS TO ASK

■ Do I know what the organisation's purpose and principles are or even where I'd find them written down?

■ Do I try to cover every conceivable eventuality when designing a system/procedure? If so, how do I respond to the accusation that complexity leads to bureaucratic responses by the organisation?

QUOTATION 29

ALFRED P. SLOAN ON THE VALUE OF MANAGEMENT BY EXCEPTION

Use this to get rid of all the reports that tell you everything is going to plan.

Alfred Pritchard Sloan (1875–1966) was an American business executive and the long-time President, Chairman and CEO of General Motors Corporation. He is credited with turning General Motors into a global player in the automotive industry.

As a busy executive, he demanded that all reports submitted to him should be short and useful. He didn't want to drown in paper or statistics. He justified this approach saying that:

> Of all business activities 99 per cent are routine . . . The entire 100 per cent can be handled by managing the 1 per cent of exceptions.
>
> **Alfred P. Sloan**

WHAT TO DO

- Ignore the stuff that is running to plan. As a manager, you're paid to stop problems arising and to sort them out quickly when they occur. You don't want to be bogged down with data that tells you nothing and stops you from identifying the areas that do need your attention. For example, you don't need to know that the wages spent to date is £350,921 if the budget to date is £351,000. It's on target. There is no indication that there is anything unusual going on. So why even look at it?

- Instead of receiving a budget report that shows every single item, ask for a report that only shows items that are under/over budget by say 3, 4 or 5 per cent. This will enable you to focus your attention on those accounts that appear to be out of sync with projections.

- There may be very good reasons why there is a difference. It may be a temporary blip that will be corrected during the next month: e.g. a one-off drop in sales in February due to a customer delaying their February purchase until March, leading to two orders in March.

- If the reason isn't obvious, you want to know what's caused the variance as soon as possible and whether it will continue. That will enable you to take corrective action quickly enough to have some impact on the following month's figures.

- But it's not just negative variances you want to know about; an underspend on essential maintenance may indicate a lack of expert staff or tight cash flows. Either way, you need to know because it poses a potential risk to future production.

- Of course, what you really hope to see is a large positive variance on an income account such as sales, fees or interest earned. When such variances occur, you want to confirm what's caused them, run with them and see to what extent you can replicate the same positive reasons on other income accounts.

- The example given above is based on a budget/actual monthly report. However, the same principles apply to any monitoring report, such as production hours, maintenance hours, unit sales, rejected work or project progress.

QUESTIONS TO ASK

- Do I know which accounts I need to keep an eye on?
- Do I receive management reports quickly enough to enable me to take corrective action that will impact on the content of the next report?

JACK WELCH ON THE THREE ESSENTIAL MEASURES OF BUSINESS

Use this to help you recognise what you must always control and monitor.

Jack Welch (b. 1935), former Chairman and CEO of General Electric, went one step further than even management by exception when he suggested that:

> There are only three measurements that tell you nearly everything you need to know about your organisation's overall performance: employee engagement, customer satisfaction and cash flow.
>
> **Jack Welch**

This quotation is directed at senior managers mostly, as it is concerned with having a broad overview of the organisation. However, it can be applied to divisions, investment centres and trading centres as well.

WHAT TO DO

- Measuring employee engagement is difficult. Often it is something that is felt or experienced rather than measured. Use management by walking about (MBWA) to take the collective pulse of the organisation or your staff. Start by defining the purpose of your walk, e.g. to determine how staff feel about a recent reorganisation. Identify where best you will get a feel for people's opinions, say production or despatch. Then off you go, but don't take a clipboard or pen. This is a listening exercise. So follow the advice given in Quotation 77 and spend at least twice as much time listening as speaking.

- Engage people in conversation. Talk about the weather, sport or what was on TV just to get a conversation going. Then start to ask questions, but keep them general. Use questions like: How have things been going since the reorganisation? Any problems with the new approach? What more do you think we need to do? Done properly, people will open up and tell you stuff that you would never hear if you remained in your office.

■ Use the feedback from customers and customer complaints to assess the level of customer satisfaction. Pay particular attention to the responses that customers provide after your staff have resolved the problem. People accept that errors occur. However, if you can quickly resolve the issue, you can actually leave the customer feeling better disposed towards your organisation than they did before the problem arose.

■ Make a point of meeting with customers and chatting to them. As with MBWA, avoid formality and try and get them to talk about what they think of your organisation, both the good and the bad. Don't become defensive if they become critical about the organisation and/or its staff. Take what they say on-board and check it out later.

■ Act on the information you collect from staff and customers. Seek to build on the positives and eliminate the negatives.

■ Ensure that you receive regular cash flow reports (see Quotation 4) and listen to your accountant. If they say that you are likely to have cash-flow problems in three months' time, take action immediately. Don't bury your head in the sand and hope it will go away. Discuss the best ways to increase receipts and reduce payments without harming essential elements of the business (see the Kaizen approach suggested in Quotation 5).

QUESTIONS TO ASK

■ Do I receive a monthly one- or two-page report on employee engagement, customer satisfaction and cash flow? If not, why not?

■ Which one of the three areas discussed above do I understand least? How can I remedy this?

QUOTATION 31 # RON DENNIS ON SUPPORTING THE WEAKEST LINK

Use this to remind you that you need to remedy the weak points in your operation.

Ron Dennis (b. 1949) is best known as the owner, CEO and Chairman of McLaren Technology Group, which runs the famous Formula 1 racing team.

Considering the ultra-competitive nature of Formula 1 racing, the following quotation can appear surprising as it posits an essentially benign and humanistic approach to management. But does it?

> The role of management is always to identify the weakest links, support them and strengthen them.
>
> **Ron Dennis**

WHAT TO DO

- Remember that in whatever team, department or organisation you run, you are only as good as your weakest link. You can't afford to carry passengers – unless your weakest link is the owner's son/daughter, in which case you can't afford not to carry them.

- Identify your weakest link. This could be a person, process or procedure. If it's a person, look to retrain them or move them to a less challenging task that they can do well. Start by carrying out a training needs analysis on the person (see Quotation 15), followed by an agreed programme of training and development. If retraining and/or redeployment doesn't work, you need to get rid of them.

- Firing someone doesn't contradict Ron Dennis's suggestion: it's merely the logical conclusion to his line of thought. You help people to improve but if they can't or won't improve you let them go. You can't run your operation well if, demonstrably, there is someone not pulling their weight. Their presence will have a negative impact on both production and staff morale as others have to rectify their mistakes. For example, I can't imagine that Ron would allow anyone who cocked-up changing a tyre during a Grand Prix twice anywhere near the pits again.

■ Involve human resources from a very early stage whenever you have a concern about someone's ability to do their job to the standard required.

■ If the weakest link is a process, procedure, machine or other inanimate object, replace it. If you can't afford to do that, find a way to minimise the impact it has on your team.

QUESTIONS TO ASK

■ How many people have I personally sacked in my career?

■ Am I capable of sacking someone?

ZIG ZIGLAR ON WHY YOU SHOULD INVEST IN STAFF TRAINING

Use this to remind you of the absolute necessity to train your staff.

Zig Ziglar (1926–2012) was an American businessman, motivational speaker and author. He recognised that some managers saw staff training as a waste of both time and money because, once trained, many staff left. He countered this argument by suggesting that:

> The only thing worse than training people and having them leave is not training people and having them stay.
>
> **Zig Ziglar**

WHAT TO DO

- Accept that any member of staff with an ounce of sense or ambition recognises that they must constantly update their skills and knowledge to remain marketable. The best will leave if you don't provide training opportunities. You will then incur the cost of recruiting and training a new person and suffering reduced productivity as they learn the job. So, in the long run, you don't save anything by not training your staff.

- Recognise that training doesn't have to be expensive. People can learn how to do a job, or do their job better, by being taught how to do it by an expert member of staff (sitting with Nelly), shadowing a member of staff or attending the free training events organised by suppliers and consultants on how to use new systems and/ or machines that they have installed. It's also feasible to arrange in-house training events given by other members of staff: e.g. what's wrong with the accountant doing a presentation for staff on, say, budgetary control?

- When staff are sent on a short course, ensure that the organisation gets value for money by agreeing with the person a set of learning objectives. When they return from the training, have them do a short training session for their colleagues. The terror of having to deliver training to colleagues on their return will mean that they pay attention while on the course and, by cascading down their learning, the unit cost of training is reduced.

When staff go on professional courses, agree to pay the fees only on successful completion of the course. If you are afraid they will leave immediately after they get their qualification, make it a condition of funding that they stay for an agreed period of time after completion of their course. One or two years is not unreasonable.

Always remember, ignorance costs money. For example, what percentage of Microsoft Office do you think the average person uses? No, I don't know either. But, when you consider the huge range of modules on undergraduate and post-graduate maths courses that are devoted to using Microsoft Excel, you get an inkling of how little is used. If your staff could use just 20 per cent more of the facilities they have on their computer systems, think of the improvement in productivity that would produce.

QUESTIONS TO ASK

What's my attitude to training staff? Do I see it as a cost or an investment?

Do I see the training I undertake as a cost or an investment?

CONCLUSION

The quality of your staff can make or break you as a manager. However selecting the right staff is extremely difficult. Managers need every bit of help they can get in this area; that's why I have chosen Warren Buffet's quotation for inclusion in the Top Ten:

> Somebody once said that in looking for people to hire, you look for three qualities: integrity, intelligence and energy. And if they don't have the first, the other two will kill you. You think about it; it's true. If you hire somebody without integrity, you really [do] want them to be dumb and lazy.
>
> **Warren Buffet**

With his customary ability to identify the crucial factor/s in any situation Buffet has identified the one key characteristic that all good staff have – integrity.

ONE LESSON TO TAKE AWAY

The overriding message that emerges from this section is that, as a manager, you need to appoint people of integrity whom you can trust. Then you need to get out of their way and let them do their job while monitoring performance through a small selection of key indicators.

SECTION 4

LEADERSHIP

INTRODUCTION

During the 1980s, managers were seen as proactive go-getters who were taking over from the mere administrators who were to blame for the state of British business. They were the new knights in shining armour riding to the rescue in their bright, shiny Porsches. By the 1990s, managers were being cast as reactive and lacking vision and the new heroes on the block were leaders.

Now the truth is that Britain didn't build an empire and win two world wars without leaders. The administrators of those days were acting as leaders just as the managers of the 1980s were leading their companies out of the stagnation of the 1970s.

What I'm saying is that leaders are not some elite band of people born with innate skills that means their destiny is to lead. They still put on their trousers or tights one leg at a time. Bear that in mind as you read the following.

This section is structured as follows. Quotation/s:

- 33 discusses the making of a leader.
- 34 to 38 outline what leaders must do.
- 39 and 40 are concerned with values and vision building.
- 41–42 provide a means for people to judge if they are acting like a leader.

As you read the entries, consider to what extent you act as a leader every day. You will probably be surprised how often you take on a leadership role. The reason for your surprise is your actions aren't heroic or visionary. That's because leadership requires a leader to do only two things: convince people that s/he is going somewhere (this might be from not achieving targets to over-achievement) and persuading them to join him/her on the journey.

QUOTATION 33 # WARREN BENNIS ON THE MAKING OF A LEADER (TOP TEN ENTRY)

Use this to remind you that with practice you can become a great leader.

Warren Bennis (1925–2014) was an American academic, management consultant and an influential writer on the subject of leadership. One of the tasks he set himself was to demystify the concept of leadership. He firmly believed that:

> The most dangerous leadership myth is that leaders are born . . . The myth asserts that people simply either have certain charismatic qualities or not. That's nonsense . . . Leaders are made rather than born.
>
> **Warren Bennis**

In his seminal book with Burt Nanus, *Leaders: Strategies For Taking Charge*, he provides pen portraits of 40 successful leaders, many of whom clearly lacked charisma as most people would understand it.

Like the old joke about the musician who asked a New Yorker, 'How do I get to Carnegie Hall?' People become leaders with practice.

WHAT TO DO

■ To become an expert in any field, Malcom Gladwell, author of *The Outliers*, suggests that you need to practise for 10,000 hours. This figure seems to hold true over a wide range of professions from science to football and from writing to medicine. Assuming a 36-hour working week, that amounts to a requirement of approximately 278 weeks or 5.34 years of work experience for a leader to become an expert. Unfortunately, you can probably double that figure because much of your time will be spent on administration, drinking coffee and attending meetings. So start to become a leader early!

■ From the day you start work, don't think of yourself as an accountant, economist, systems analyst or the member of any other trade or profession. Think of yourself as a leader and act accordingly. Record your success and failures in your learning journal and analyse the reason for both.

■ Read about leadership. Vary your reading between textbooks, leadership guides and biographies of great leaders. This provides the fuel for your thinking about leadership.

■ Arrange to shadow a leader you respect in your organisation for a couple of months on a part-time basis – you still have to do the day job. If that isn't possible, observe the actions of those people in the organisation who you and others think of as leaders. These people may not be members of senior management. They might be supervisors or middle managers. In your learning journal, record how they, and other leaders, deal with specific situations. Analyse what they did, and try to identify the ideas and strategies that they used.

■ Whether you are a senior, middle or junior manager, volunteer to lead projects, especially those requiring cross-departmental co-operation. Project management will provide you with experience of dealing with a range of issues, people and disciplines, many of which will be outside your normal professional experience. You may find it difficult, but as a developmental experience it's invaluable.

■ Don't be put off if people tell you you're not a leader. What they really mean is that you are not their kind of leader. Mrs Thatcher was loathed and despised by large sections of the British public, but no one could deny that she was a leader.

QUESTIONS TO ASK

■ Do I think of myself as a leader? If not, why not?
■ Who's the best leader I've ever worked for? What were the characteristics I admired most about their style of leadership?

HOWARD D. SCHULTZ ON WHY LEADERS MUST PROVIDE FOLLOWERS WITH MEANING AND PURPOSE

Use this to remind you of what your followers want.

Howard D. Schultz (b. 1953) is Chairman and CEO of Starbucks. In the following quotation he addresses the fundamental question of why people give their loyalty to an organisation and/or leaders:

> [People] want to be part of something they're really proud of, that they will fight for, sacrifice for, that they trust.
>
> **Howard Schultz**

WHAT TO DO

- If you want to be a successful leader, you need to energise staff by providing them with a purpose. Most commentators call this a vision for the organisation that people can buy into (see Quotation 40). People need to believe that what they do is meaningful and that they are not wasting their life turning up for work each day. I left the best paid job I ever had and took a significant reduction in salary to move from an organisation that manufactured labels to one that housed people. It was the best decision I ever made. My new job had meaning for me.
- The Hawthorne Experiments of the 1920s and 30s demonstrated that not wanting to let their colleagues down, and indeed gaining their respect, was a major factor in motivating staff. A second significant feature was management taking an interest in what each member of staff was doing and thinking.
- Providing a purpose, encouraging team working and managers showing a genuine interest in each member of staff provides the conditions required for staff to feel:
  - that they belong;
  - are valued as individuals;
  - pride in what they do, the people they do it with and the organisation they do it for.

- The chocolate manufacturer Cadbury's had a reputation for just such traits when it was still run by the Cadbury family. To work at Cadbury's was a badge of honour in Birmingham that all staff wore with pride. The result was a highly motivated and loyal workforce.

- Finally, a leader needs to build a reputation for honesty and integrity (see Quotation 25). The commitment of staff to Cadbury's was particularly strong because it was based on the unwavering belief that the Cadbury family had their best interests at heart and would always treat them with consideration, fairness and frankness. If you can build a similar trust with your followers, you will have a workforce willing to follow you anywhere.

QUESTIONS TO ASK

- What purpose/vision do I have for my team, department or organisation?

- How much time do I spend talking to staff about their job, frustrations and aspirations?

PETER DRUCKER ON WHY RESULTS MAKE LEADERS

Use this as the only true measure of your leadership ability.

Peter Drucker (1919–2005) was never afraid to ruffle a few feathers. While many writers were talking about how great managers were required to be charismatic and/or transformational, Drucker cut through the hype and said that:

> Effective leadership is not about making speeches or being liked; leadership is defined by results not attributes.
>
> **Peter Drucker**

Effectively, what Drucker claimed was that leaders are defined by the results not personal characteristics. If you achieve outstanding results, people will view you as a great leader. They will even start to analyse your leadership style and try and identify the secrets of your success for others to use.

WHAT TO DO

- You cannot demand that people call you their glorious leader, unless you have the military and the secret police to back you up. The title of leader is bestowed on you by your followers. To attract followers you have to demonstrate achievements. Once you do that, people will want to be associated with you and the work you do because they, too, want to be part of something bigger than themselves that is successful (see Quotation 34).

- Manage expectations. Always underpromise and overdeliver. Never accept an unrealistic deadline. Such deadlines set you up to fail. Instead, negotiate the deadline with your boss. For example, you're asked to run a project and your boss suggests that it will take only six weeks. Play for time. Say something like, 'Can I have a couple of days to think about how I'm going to handle it?.' A reasonable boss will have no problems with that. Assess the job fully and decide how long you think you need. If it's seven weeks, you go back to your boss and say you need eight weeks. You then deliver in seven. That way you are the manager who delivers ahead of the deadline and not the one who was a week late (see Quotation 79).

■ If the deadline is immovable, still play for time, only this time review the workload contained in the project. Identify the 80 per cent plus of the work that you can do in the time available. Normally, this will be sufficient to satisfy the organisation's requirements. The less urgent aspects of the project can then be delivered after the deadline.

■ For all targets, both those that are delegated to you and those you draw up for your staff, describe and define them using the SMART criteria (see Quotation 19), i.e. each target must be specific, measurable, achievable, realistic and timely.

■ Hold regular review meetings with staff to monitor progress against each target. Where there is a significant negative variance from that expected, take corrective action; where there is a positive variance, identify what has caused it and see whether it can be extended further.

QUESTIONS TO ASK

■ Am I a pushover when it comes to accepting deadlines or do I negotiate fair but challenging deadlines with my bosses?

■ How effective am I at monitoring progress against my targets?

QUOTATION 36 # WARREN BENNIS ON WHY LEADERS MUST WALK THE TALK

Use this to remind you that to be leader you must be yourself. You can't fake it.

Warren Bennis (1925–2014) spent much of his academic career trying to discover the secret of leadership. He probably came closest in the following two quotations:

> Leaders walk their talk; in true leaders there is no gap between the theories they espouse and their practice.
>
> Becoming a leader is synonymous with becoming yourself. It is precisely that simple, and it is also that difficult.
>
> **Warren Bennis**

As Bennis implies in his first quotation, being genuine, being consistent in your words and actions is hellishly difficult to achieve. Even though you may not achieve it all the time, it should still be your aim.

WHAT TO DO

- Remember, people follow those they trust and they trust those who are consistent and predictable. It's extremely difficult to gain people's trust in the first place but one misstep and you can lose it. People want their leaders to be special and they place them on a pedestal as someone to admire and support. However, if they see any mismatch between what a leader says and does, they see it as a betrayal of their trust, and disillusionment quickly sets in.

- Work out what principles will guide your professional life. Don't have too many of them. A principle in this context is something you would be willing to resign over. If you are not willing to resign over a matter, then your firmly held belief is just a position you hold until it becomes inconvenient, at which point you dump it.

- As in Quotation 35, work to lower expectations. Don't try and develop a public image that is pristine and perfect. Be honest with people and talk openly about both your strengths and weaknesses as a leader. For example, unless you are a production engineer by training, you might say, 'I have a good understanding of the issues facing our production team, but that's not enough. That's why I always seek the advice of our engineers on technical matters.'

- If you try to pretend that you understand issues when you clearly don't, any credibility you have will be shot to pieces. Never be afraid to ask a question or say, 'I'm sorry I don't understand.' It will encourage others to do the same.

- Never break your word or renege on a deal, even if it costs the organisation money. Word will get round and any losses will be recouped in the future in both cash and goodwill.

- Never take credit for someone else's work or idea.

- Treat people as you would like to be treated, i.e. as a human being and not just a resource to be used and discarded (see Quotation 26).

QUESTIONS TO ASK

- Do I walk the talk?
- Do staff trust me? If not, why not?

QUOTATION 37   # EDWARD DEMING ON BUILDING CREDIBILITY WITH FOLLOWERS

Use this to help you build credibility with your staff.

Edward Deming (1900–93) was the foremost authority on quality improvement in the second half of the twentieth century. A fierce critic of management, which he thought was responsible for over 90 per cent of all the problems, he argued that:

> To manage one must lead. To lead, one must understand the work that he and his people are responsible for.
>
> **Edward Deming**

One of the most pernicious lies about leaders is that, if they can lead a factory, they are equally capable of leading a fashion house because leadership skills are generic and therefore transferable. What rubbish. Leaders must have credibility with their followers if they are to be respected and trusted. Staff will always be suspicious of someone who lacks knowledge about the sector they are working in. In such situations the 'wannabe' leader can exercise power and force change through but they will never have any followers.

The same problem exists when a leader moves from one organisation to another, even if it's within the same sector.

New leaders must learn about their organisation, its history, norms of practice and its culture if they are to be successful and even then they may not be accepted.

WHAT TO DO

- Depending on the number of staff you manage, either find the time to sit with each person individually or select a sample and talk to them. Don't hold the meeting in your office. Go to where they work and let them tell you about what they do and the problems they face.

- Get a feel for the environment in which the person works. Is it a mad house with phones ringing and constant interruptions or a haven of tranquillity?

- Spend about an hour or so with each person selected.

- Try to share the staff's experience of the job. Robert Townsend insisted that everyone who worked for Avis Rent a Car must spend two weeks on the car rental desk at a busy airport – no exceptions. He recounts how some senior executives panicked and ran away from customers. Politically elected officials with no experience of the service they are leading should be required to spend time working with front-line staff.

- As you move about the organisation, keep your eyes open and note down anything that strikes you as odd, interesting or unusual. Ask a colleague or trusted member of staff about what you have observed.

- Use meetings as a way to observe how the organisation operates. For example, is it democratic or do one or two powerful individuals run things?

- Use management by walking about (MBWA) as a way to maintain contact and build relationships and knowledge (see Quotation 30) with the wider staff.

- If you are entirely new to the sector, consider having an experienced member of staff shadow you for, say, two or three months. They can discreetly advise you about what passes for normal procedure and/ or behavioural norms, and their feedback on how you acted can accelerate your learning.

QUESTIONS TO ASK

- How much do I know about what my staff actually do and the problems they face?

- Could I list three major cultural norms that underpin my organisation's behaviour?

QUOTATION 38 # HENRY MINTZBERG ON WHY LEADERSHIP IS MANAGEMENT PRACTISED WELL

Use this to remind you that management and leadership are not two distinct functions.

Canadian-born academic and writer Henry Mintzberg (b. 1939) has written widely on a range of management subjects. In recent years he has argued against the idea that management and leadership are two separate functions:

> Leadership cannot simply delegate management; instead of distinguishing managers from leaders, we should be seeing managers as leaders and leadership as management practised well.
>
> **Henry Minzberg**

WHAT TO DO

- Instead of setting up a list of traits/actions for leaders and posing them as opposites to management, Mintzberg sees each as existing on a continuum. Where on the continuum you exist at any one time determines whether you are managing or leading.

The management leadership spectrum

Managers are concerned with . . . ◄─►	*Leaders are concerned with . . .*
The present	The future
Plans	Vision
Maintenance of systems	The big picture
Maintaining the status quo	Change
Feedback	Inspiration
Objectives	Outcomes
Monitoring and controlling staff	Exercising influence over followers
Providing a sense of order	Providing a sense of purpose and direction for followers
Spreading organisational culture	Building organisational culture
Doing things right	Doing the right things

Managers are concerned with . . . ⟷	Leaders are concerned with . . .
Dealing with complexity within and around the organisation	Dealing with change and the effects of change
Producing order and consistency	Producing change and movement
Planning and budgeting	Vision building and strategising
Organisational structure and staffing	Aligning people behind a common vision or set of objectives
Problem solving	Problem identification in advance and eradication at source
Economy and efficiency	Effectiveness
Staying on the right path	Making new paths

Adapted from McGrath, J. (2004) 'Leading in a managerialist paradigm: a survey of perceptions within a faculty of education'. Doctoral thesis: University of Birmingham.

- Stop thinking of yourself as a manager or a leader. Rather, think of yourself as an actor playing a role. Sometimes you will need to be a manager, focused entirely on the present as you try to overcome a short-term problem and meet an urgent deadline. At other times you will need to provide your staff with a vision of where you see the team, department or organisation going in the next five years. Both are roles that you play, and the ability to play them resides within all of us.

- However, while we all have the potential to lead, only those who are willing to leave the relative safety of management behind and strike out on their own to become a leader will succeed. Leadership is a lonely and risky business. You are leaving the herd and management team behind and saying, 'I know what we need to do. Follow me.' Not everyone has the self-confidence and ego to do that. However, if you want it badly enough, you can develop your self-belief just as you can develop your management and leadership skills (see Quotations 14 and 15).

QUESTIONS TO ASK

- The buck always stops with the leader. Am I willing to accept that ultimate responsibility?
- Leaders sometimes have to say the unsayable. Am I willing to express unpopular views at work and in my social life and live with the consequences?

QUOTATION 39

S.K. CHAKRABORTY ON THE SOURCE OF ORGANISATIONAL VALUES

Use this to help you identify or develop the organisations values.

S.K. Chakraborty (b. 1957) is an Indian academic and writer who has written extensively on business ethics and values. He suggests that:

> Organisational values always derive from individual values – especially those of the founding fathers and of the top executives.
>
> **S.K. Chakraborty**

As a leader you have a role to play in creating, upholding and spreading the organisation's values.

WHAT TO DO

- A useful starting point is to find out what the organisation's values are. This may be relatively simple or be so difficult that finding them would defeat the combined efforts of Colombo, Poirot, Morse and Rebus.
- Check to see whether there is an organisational values statement. If there is, treat it with some scepticism until you have had the opportunity to see those values in operation within the company. During this period of observation, note down the values that you see or don't see displayed.
- If there is no written set of values, check to see whether there is a vision statement and/or a mission statement. Normally, both documents are underpinned by the organisation's values, even if they aren't stated overtly. Again, don't necessarily believe what you find. Observe how the organisation treats its employees, customers, suppliers, shareholders and other stakeholders. This can tell you a lot. For example, if you're at a meeting and some poor soul is being ritually humiliated in public, then whatever the espoused values are, the organisation does not respect its staff.
- If you can find no documentary evidence of values, don't assume that the organisation doesn't have strong values. I doubt very much

that Cadbury's ever drew up a values statements when it was run by the Cadbury family. Everyone knew its values were based on Quaker philosophy and these were on display in everything it did.

- If you can discover nothing written down, simply observe and speak to colleagues about what they think the organisation's values are.
- If you find that the organisation doesn't have any values to guide it or if they are ignored, then, depending on your seniority, you have a decision to make. A middle or junior manager can't impose their values on the organisation. A senior manager can, provided they get the backing of the senior management team and/or board. Of course, if you are the Chair (wo)man or CEO, you can start to change the organisation's culture, but make sure that you have considered how you will deal with opposition to your ideas (see Quotations 61 and 63).
- In the absence of organisational values, it is possible to manage your own staff according to a set of values that you believe in. They may even spread to other parts of the organisation.
- Remember, values are about how you act not what you say. They need to be absorbed by the staff and acted out unconsciously in everything they do. Only when staff uphold organisational values when no one is watching can you claim success.
- Remember, if you don't stand for something, you'll end up standing for anything.

QUESTIONS TO ASK

- What values do I have to guide me as a person and a manager?
- Do I know what the organisation's values are and what role I'm expected to play in upholding them?

QUOTATION 40 # CLAUDE I. TAYLOR ON VISION BUILDING

Use this to help you communicate and disseminate your vision to staff.

Claude I. Taylor (1925–2015) was Chairman of Air Canada for a number of years. He observed that:

> Certainly a leader needs a clear vision of the organisation and where it's going, but a vision is of little value unless it is shared in a way to generate enthusiasm and commitment. Leadership and communication are inseparable.
>
> **Claude I. Taylor**

WHAT TO DO

- Too many vision statements are a load of pious pap. A vision statement is not the same as a mission statement, objective or target. It's something that the organisation aspires to. It's something you would like the organisation to be or represent. You may never get there but it's what keeps the organisation moving forward. That means that it has to be meaningful, clear, understandable and easy to communicate to staff, customers and other stakeholders.

- Unfortunately, too many organisations produce long-winded statements that are difficult to understand and hard to remember. They then compound these errors when they fail to share the vision with staff in a way that people can understand. Sticking a copy of the vision statement up all round the place just isn't going to cut it. Left to their own devices, a group of 20 people will all interpret differently what a statement means and will have difficulty relating it to their job.

- Use the following strategy to ensure that all staff understand and sign up to the statement:

  - Write the mission statement in clear simple English without any jargon or management speak.
  - Keep writing and rewriting the statement until you have distilled your message down to fewer than 20 words.

- Arrange a series of staff briefings at which you introduce the statement and explain what management mean by it. No matter how simple and clear your statement is, this is essential. Why? Because what senior management understand by certain words means something else to staff down the hierarchy. For example, 'efficient delivery of services' means maximising outputs from a given input to management but a reduction in staff to front-line staff.

- Allow staff to ask questions, and answer them truthfully. Don't be afraid to tell someone that they have misunderstood the statement if they have, but be open to the possibility that the statement is ambiguous.

- Don't wait for staff to ask, 'How does my job contribute to achieving/moving closer to the vision?' Tell them how important their work is. Give them multiple simple examples of how different jobs contribute to the vision. For example, you can produce a great product but, if they are carelessly packaged by staff and damaged in transit, customers are not going to be happy.

- Leaders and managers need to continually refer to the vision statement in their daily work. When there is a problem, people should automatically think, 'What's the best way to deal with this in line with our vision statement?' If that means ignoring procedures or processes, so be it. No one should be criticised for prioritising the vision statement over petty rules and regulation.

QUESTIONS TO ASK

- Can I recite the organisation's vision word for word? Can my staff paraphrase the vision statement?
- Am I cynical about the value of the vision statement? If so, how does this affect my staff's attitude to it?

QUOTATION 41   # DORIS KEARNS GOODWIN ON WHY LEADERS NEED PEOPLE TO DISAGREE WITH THEM

Use this to elicit ideas from all those around you.

Doris Kearns Goodwin (b. 1943) is an American biographer, historian and political commentator. She argues that by listening to a diverse range of opinions a leader can increase significantly the quality of their decision making:

> Good leadership requires you to surround yourself with people of diverse perspectives who can disagree with you without fear of retaliation.
>
> **Doris Kearns Goodwin**

WHAT TO DO

- Recognise that you are biased. We all are. Based on our past experiences and upbringing, we have opinions on a multitude of issues, many of which we know next to nothing about. When faced with a decision, these opinions form part of your thinking at either a conscious or subconscious level. You need people around you to question and challenge your prefabricated ideas, expose your prejudices and make you think anew.

- The problem is that such people are as rare as hens' gold teeth. The reason they are so rare is because, in many organisations, whenever they raise their head above the parapet and disagree with their boss, it gets shot off. Many managers and leaders say, 'I don't want yes people around me', only to prove at the very next meeting they hold that they hate to be challenged and will slap down any poor soul who has the temerity to disagree with them. Serial offenders are banished to a cold little gulag in a distant part of the organisation for re-education and are allowed to reappear in public only when they can repeat, convincingly, statements such as, 'I couldn't agree more' and 'That's a wonderful idea'.

- A strong leader is not afraid of constructive dissent from staff and colleagues. So encourage people to challenge your ideas and views. Don't dismiss other people's arguments out of hand. Evaluate them fairly and be willing to change your mind if need be. If you decide to reject a suggestion or recommendation, be willing to explain the reasons for your decision.

- By showing you will not decapitate people who disagree with you or hold grudges against them, you are opening up the possibility of genuine dialogue between you and your colleagues and staff.

- The influx of new ideas from people who are not afraid to question their boss, authority, received wisdom or the status quo is one of the great untapped resources of business. If you can access it, it will make you a more successful leader in the eyes of the world because results will improve (see Quotation 45), and a great leader in the hearts and minds of your staff because you listen, show them respect and motivate them by giving them the freedom to change how they work.

QUESTIONS TO ASK

- When challenged at a meeting, do I become defensive, aggressive or interested in what the person has to say?

- Do I always have to be in charge at a meeting? Should I take a back seat more often and just listen to what people are saying?

QUOTATION 42 # JOHN QUINCY ADAMS ON HOW YOU KNOW YOU ARE A LEADER

Use this as a way to evaluate your impact on followers.

John Quincy Adams (1767–1848) was a statesman and sixth President of the United States of America. His definition of a leader is predicated on the effect that they have on their followers. Thus:

> If your actions inspire others to dream more, learn more, do more and become more, you are a leader.
>
> **John Quincy Adams**

WHAT TO DO

- Followers are not just inspired by what leaders achieve. They are inspired by the leader's story. Did they become successful by being ruthless, driven and greedy like Gordon Gekko in *Wall Street,* or did they become the biggest man in town by always putting the needs of others first, like George Bailey in *It's a Wonderful Life?* In other words, people are influenced by the leader's character and values. If people buy into your actions, values and character, then you are well on the way to becoming a leader.

- Words can also inspire and lift people. Both Churchill and Martin Luther King used language to inspire their followers during the darkest of times. But those words would have sounded flat and meaningless if their actions did not match what they said. Despite the danger, Churchill stayed in London throughout the Second World War, and Martin Luther King placed himself at the front of many marches knowing that he ran the risk of being attacked by police and their dogs, state troopers and 'concerned citizens', including the Klu Klux Klan. If your words match your actions, then people will trust and follow you.

- How you deliver the message is a difficult one. Churchill and Martin Luther King were great orators. Both of them had studied oratory and were experts at structuring their speeches for maximum effect and coining phrases that will never be forgotten as long as English is spoken. You don't have to be a great orator. You just need to communicate with your followers using clear, simple words and unambiguous statements. However, what you say must be said with sincerity. You have to believe it. If you do, then listeners will hear it in your voice. Don't be afraid of a bit of emotion. It shows people that you care, that what you are saying means something to you; it makes you more human and draws your listeners in.

- Don't forget that people are judged by how they look (see Quotation 13). When you are starting out, you probably need to conform to the accepted dress code in your organisation, which may be a dark suit/dress or tee shirt and jeans. As you become successful, you can adopt a style that suits you. This will become part of your image, which people associate with you, and will not detract from the message you are delivering. It may even enhance it.

- Don't be afraid to try and inspire people. People want to be inspired/swept away.

QUESTIONS TO ASK

- How consistent are my actions with what I say?
- In my life, who has inspired me? What was it about them that I found inspiring?

CONCLUSION

There was strong competition for the accolade of Top Ten entry in this section between Warren Bennis and Henry Mintzberg. Both of them are seeking to undermine the myth that leaders are born not made and that they possess special gifts. It's important to destroy this *canard* if we are to develop enough leaders to take us forward in both the private and public sectors. I finally chose Warren Bennis's quotation as it is simple, clear and carries greater force:

> The most dangerous leadership myth is that leaders are born ... The myth asserts that people simply either have certain charismatic qualities or not. That's nonsense ... Leaders are made rather than born.
>
> **Warren Bennis**

If you are still not convinced that leadership has little to do with special people who possess extraordinary abilities, consider the following quotation I found while researching this book. It's the only quotation I've used that has its origins in a committee:

> The crux of leadership is that you must constantly stop to consider how your decisions will influence people.
>
> **Michigan State Police maxim**

This is a much more achievable definition of leadership and is an approach that anyone can apply.

ONE LESSON TO TAKE AWAY

The lesson I would like you to take away from this section must be pretty obvious already. Everyone can be a leader, including you. You just have to step up to the plate and give it a try.

SECTION 5

MOTIVATION

INTRODUCTION

My respect for Peter Drucker will be obvious to anyone who has read this book. I, along with many others, think he is the most important writer on management science that has ever lived. Therefore, it was with some trepidation that I stared to write this section because Drucker said:

> We know nothing about motivation. All we can do is write books about it.
>
> **Peter Drucker**

Now, I agree with Drucker. I'm not even sure if all motivation is innate and that what we call motivation by managers simply influences the flow of motivation within a person or group rather than creates it. (There are several potential PhDs in that last sentence and, no, I'm not in the market to do one.)

What follows is an attempt to catch a glimpse of this slippery concept from different angles. The section is structured as follows. Quotation/s:

- 43 deals with how in many (most?) organisations, management institutionally treats adults like children.
- 44 and 45 explore how people need their work to be meaningful.
- 46 and 47 consider how self-motivation can be encouraged by managers.
- 48 suggests that, as in so much else, a kind word can have a huge impact on a person's motivation.

As you read this section, consider which approaches to motivation you currently use and which you would feel comfortable using in the future.

QUOTATION 43

ROBERT FROST ON DISENCHANTMENT IN THE WORKPLACE

Use this to remind you to treat staff as intelligent functioning adults.

Robert Lee Frost (1874–1963) was an American poet and four-time winner of the Pulitzer Prize for Poetry. His poems often dealt with the trials and tribulations of ordinary working people. His great observational skills of people at work are captured in the following quotation.

> The brain is a wonderful organ; it starts the moment you get up in the morning and does not stop until you get into the office
>
> **Robert Frost**

Contained within the humour is a plea for management at all levels to recognise that workers are not automatons but intelligent, thinking human beings who, outside of work, buy a house, raise/manage a family, work to a budget, plan for the future and run or take part in all sorts of activities that require commitment and often good management skills, e.g. directing amateur dramatics productions, running a band, volunteering in hospitals and hospices, the list is endless.

Unfortunately, when they arrive at work, they are treated as if they are children: their every act proscribed by a process or procedure and any suggestions they make ignored because of a 'what do they know?' attitude from management. Is it any wonder that they switch off 90 per cent of their brain as soon as they get to work and become apathetic and despondent?

'Well, I won't need you for the next 8 hours'

WHAT TO DO

- Stop the infantilisation of your staff. Now! Treat them like intelligent human beings who have much to contribute to the organisation if they are given a chance (see Quotation 45).

- Involve staff in the decision-making process (see Quotation 54). How far you take this is up to you but, at an absolute minimum, when you are making a decision that affects your staff or the work they do, you should collect their views on the subject.

- Encourage staff to become leaders (see Quotation 33). In any football team, there is the team captain but managers are constantly talking about the need for numerous players to be 'real leaders on the field'. The same multi-leadership approach is required at work.

- Show staff how important their job is to the organisation and how their efforts contribute to the firm's overall success (see Quotation 44).

- Use Herzberg's insights to motivate staff (see Quotation 45). In particular, supply every person with at least some interesting and challenging tasks to perform as part of their workload. This may mean redistributing some of the mundane jobs among staff. In addition, always recognise when someone has produced good work.

- Communicate regularly with staff. Listen actively to their ideas about how to improve customer service (see Section 10). In addition, ask about the problems they face and talk through possible resolutions. Follow up on the issues raised and ensure that they are properly assessed and corrective action taken.

QUESTIONS TO ASK

- Do I switch the whole or part of my brain off when I arrive at work?
- How good am I at recognising the extent to which skills that I and my staff use outside of work could be transferred into the workplace?

QUOTATION 44 # KENNETH AND SCOTT BLANCHARD ON EXPLAINING TO PEOPLE WHY THEIR WORK IS IMPORTANT

Use this to help you get the message across to staff that their work is important.

Kenneth Blanchard (b. 1939) is most famous for the model of Situational Leadership that he developed with Paul Hersey. He runs his own leadership consultancy where Scott Blanchard works as a lecturer and key note speaker.

In a world where many of us are just a cog in a large machine, very few of us are able to see a job through from start to finish. This makes it difficult for staff to see how they contribute to the 'finished article', whatever that may be. Ken and Scott Blanchard suggest that managers need to:

> Connect the dots between individual roles and the goals of the organisation. When people see that connection, they get a lot of energy out of work. They feel the importance, dignity and meaning in their job.
>
> **Ken Blanchard and Scott Blanchard**

WHAT TO DO

- If it's not clear what contribution your team makes to the overall success of the organisation, draw up an organisational process map.
- This is not the same as an organisation chart; rather, it is a mind map showing how achievement of your team's targets and objectives flow through the organisation. Think of your contribution as a small tributary flowing into a larger tributary, and so on, until it reaches the main river which empties into the sea. This meeting of the river and sea is the point at which the organisation achieves its stated aims and objectives.
- You don't have to show how other teams and departments contribute to the organisation's end result. You just want to show how your team's efforts contribute to the whole. So keep it simple and paint it with broad brush strokes. Add For example:

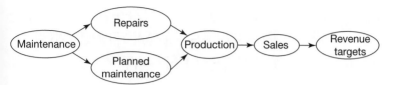

- Once you are happy with your river map, present it to the staff and emphasise what an essential part they play in the organisation and how a failure on their part affects the organisation as a whole. You might want to over-egg the pudding in this context and build up the importance of their contribution to final results.
- After you've made your pitch, ask all staff to map how their work and achievement feed into the team's targets and objectives. It's surprising how few members of staff actually understand how their work contributes to their own team's overall achievements. This is particularly the case in large departments/teams.
- Discuss each person's mind map with them and correct any misunderstandings and emphasise, again, the value of what they do to the team and the organisation.
- As a general policy, always emphasise the importance of the work your team does both to staff and colleagues. Your aim is to establish a pervasive feeling in the minds of your staff and others that the work they do is important.

QUESTIONS TO ASK

- Do I fully understand how my work and that of my team feeds into the organisation's aims and objectives?
- How aware are my staff of their contribution to the work and wellbeing of the organisation?

QUOTATION 45 | # FREDRICK HERZBERG ON THE SOURCES OF MOTIVATION (TOP TEN ENTRY)

Use this to help you create the conditions where staff can motivate themselves.

Fredrick Herzberg (1923–2000) was a renowned academic and writer in the field of management studies. He was particularly interested in the factors that motivated people and those that didn't. One of his most surprising findings was that pay is not the great motivator that many people think it is:

> True motivation comes from achievement, personal development, job satisfaction and recognition.
>
> **Frederick Herzberg**

Herzberg identified a range of factors that had an effect on motivation. Those factors that positively motivated staff he called Motivational Factors. Those that demotivated staff if they fell below an expected standard he christened Hygiene Factors, i.e.:

Factors that motivate staff	*Factors that demotivate staff if inadequate*
Interesting work that challenges the individual.	The working environment and/ or general staff facilities such as canteens or communication with management.
Work that is meaningful to the individual and which they value.	Pay and job security when they fall below an acceptable level or are threatened.
The autonomy and discretion to arrange their work as they choose and enough resources to carry out their work.	The organisation's rules, policies and procedures when they obstruct rather than help staff.

Factors that motivate staff	Factors that demotivate staff if inadequate
Recognition of their achievements by management. The possibility of advancement which may involve promotion or being given more complex work to do.	Poor staff relations.

WHAT TO DO

- You can't motivate those who have no personal pride and don't care. Aim to recruit committed, enthusiastic and self-motivated individuals who take pride in themselves and their work (see Quotation 46).

- Use every opportunity, including general conversations, all forms of meetings, training events and social gatherings to learn as much as you can about your staff. The more you know, the better you will be at identifying what motivates them and what annoys them.

- Continually monitor the hygiene factors and ensure that none of them falls below acceptable levels.

- Ensure that everyone has a good mixture of mundane, but essential, tasks and interesting work to do. Don't give all the boring stuff to one person. If necessary, redistribute some work among staff. It would be good for team spirit if you did a bit of grunt work yourself. But limit the amount (see Quotation 20).

- Explain to staff the importance of the work they do (see Quotation 44).

- Negotiate and agree a set of targets for each member of staff. Delegate responsibility to each person for completion of their work and the discretion to do it as they see fit. Then hold them to account (see Quotation 68).

- Remember to praise good work publicly. People may feel embarrassed but that doesn't mean they don't want the recognition.

QUESTIONS TO ASK

- Do I motivate myself or do I find motivation in the words and actions of others?

- What have I tried to do to motivate my staff? Did I take personal differences into account when I tried to motivate them?

TOM PETERS ON SELF-MOTIVATION

Use this to remind you of the limited, but vital, role that managers play in motivating staff.

Tom Peters (b. 1942) worked as a Kinsey management consultant before becoming a hugely successful and influential management guru and best-selling author of several management books. He likes to think outside the box and argues that only people can motivate themselves.

> The common wisdom is that . . . managers have to learn how to motivate people. Nonsense. Employees bring their own motivation.
>
> **Tom Peters**

Peters' stance is part of the long-standing argument about the nature of motivation: i.e. is motivation intrinsic or extrinsic? Assuming he is at least partially right in his belief, what should you do?

WHAT TO DO

- Don't abandon entirely your attempts to motivate staff. Follow the advice of Fredrick Herzberg and create the conditions in which people can motivate themselves (see Quotation 45).

- In your career you will have come across people who are clearly self-motivated. Usually, the problem you have with them is controlling and channelling their energies. Others seem to believe in a fair day's work for a week's pay. To avoid this problem, you need to be able to identify the signs of self-motivation, especially when you are appointing and/or promoting staff.

- All selection processes, including interviews, are a poor predictor of how well a person will do in a specific job. The risks are reduced if it's possible to promote from within. By doing so, you reduce the risk of appointing someone who has the motivation of a sloth on a rest day. You already know the person, you know what they can do and, based on that, you can make an informed prediction of how well they will perform when promoted.

- Whether you appoint an internal or external candidate, ensure that:
  - S/he has personal pride. Such people are generally their own harshest critic and have high standards. They won't want to let themselves down and, by extension, you.
  - The person is self-motivated. This is almost assured if the candidate has high standards, as they will continually want to maintain and exceed them, if possible.
  - The appointee is enthusiastic and trustworthy. Enthusiasm should be on display in how they answer your questions and engage you in conversation about the organisation. As for trustworthiness, you'll need to obtain references for external applicants and a line manager's report for internal candidates.
  - They can see the bigger picture. This is the prime indicator of a person's suitability for senior management posts. Executives and others must be able to leave behind their own professional training and socialisation and see issues in organisational terms and not as an accountant, engineer or marketing manager.
- Finally, look to see whether they possess common sense. As we all know, it's the most uncommon trait of all but is also the foundation of good management and all that goes with it.

QUESTIONS TO ASK

- Do I think that people motivate themselves or do I believe that I have to motivate and drive them?
- If staff do motivate themselves, what impact would my driving them have on how they feel?

GENERAL GEORGE PATTON ON MOTIVATION THROUGH DELEGATION

Use this with people you trust.

General George Smith Patton, Jr (1885–1945), United States Army, was probably the most aggressive of all allied generals in the Second World War and the one the German Army feared most.

He expected and got high standards from his men and felt confident enough of their ability to say this:

> Never tell people how to do things. Tell them what to do and they will surprise you with their ingenuity.
>
> **General George Patton**

WHAT TO DO

- Part of the reason General Patton could make the above statement with assurance was that he didn't suffer fools gladly. If you were an officer under his command, you either came up to standard or he shipped you out. No excuses and no delay. He only wanted to work with the best, because he believed he was the best. In Quotations 25 and 46, advice is given on how to select the best staff available. However, even if you follow it to the letter, the chances are you will have the odd failure. When that happens, follow all the correct procedures but get them out of your team. This can be time-consuming but the remaining staff will quickly recognise that you want only the best and will raise their game. Their self-confidence will grow and they will do everything they can not to let themselves, you or their colleagues down.

- Having created a team of proud, high performers, they are not going to be stymied by an instruction from you, such as, 'I want you to do X and tell me when you've finished.' They'll see it as a sign of the trust you have in them and will welcome the opportunity to impress. Because they will put all their energies into the job, they are very likely to come up with better solutions, ideas or results than if you'd told them how to do the job. Why am I so sure of this? Simple. You don't have the time to expend all your energies on trying to come up with the best answer/result for every problem that lands on your desk. Therefore, any instructions you gave would be based on a cursory review and would limit their actions as they tried to follow the tramlines you had set down for them.

- When you implement their idea, make sure that you give the person credit for the work; this will enhance their self-confidence and faith in you as a leader further.

- Quotation 46 suggests that only people can motivate themselves. Patton's approach seems to recognise this. He created the conditions, including an expectation of excellence, which enabled staff to motivate themselves.

QUESTIONS TO ASK

- Who in my team can I trust to surprise me with their ingenuity?
- Do I have the confidence to relinquish control to my staff?

QUOTATION 48 # JOHN WOODEN ON WHY YOU NEED TO SHOW YOU CARE

Use this to remind you of the power of praise and thanks in the workplace.

John Wooden (1910–2010) was an American basketball player and coach who won the NCAA Championship ten times, including a record seven in a row. Many of the ideas he espoused were adopted by businesses in the USA, including his Pyramid of Success. One of his most oft-repeated quotations is:

> Seek opportunities to show you care. The smallest gestures often make the biggest difference.
>
> **John Wooden**

Sounds simple, but when was the last time that your boss said 'Well done' to you? Indeed, when was the last time you said it to a member of your staff? And while we're at it, what about thanking staff for good work?

WHAT TO DO

- Use every opportunity you can to get to know and understand your staff. These include daily conversations, meetings, encounters when out walking the job, over lunch, at social events and anything else you can think of. Learn about their job, the problems they face, what they like and dislike about their work. The more you demonstrate an interest in your staff and a genuine understanding of the pressures they work under, the more they will value your praise.

- When you catch someone doing something good, remark on it immediately. Everything we know about feedback tells us that the nearer to the event that feedback is given, the more powerful its impact. However, if you see someone doing something wrong, wait until the person is alone and have a quiet word. Public humiliation doesn't work!

- Just because you said 'Well done' when you saw something doesn't mean that you can't refer to it again at a staff meeting. People may feel a bit embarrassed about receiving praise in public but secretly they will be glowing inside.

- If someone is going through a tough time at work or at home, let them know you care. A simple enquiry about how a sick relative is and/or an offer to let them work from home while a loved one is sick helps cement your relationship with them.
- If something good is happening in their lives, such as a family member gaining a qualification, or news that they are about to become a parent or grandparent, celebrate their good news.
- 'Thank you' is also a powerful phrase. Just think of the last time you let someone out when driving and they didn't indicate their thanks. It's annoying. So is going the extra mile at work and no one recognising your efforts – which has happened to all of us.

QUESTIONS TO ASK

- How good am I at showing that I care for my staff as people?
- How much do I know about the lives of my staff?

CONCLUSION

My choice of the motivation entry for the Top Ten probably shows my bias. Herzberg's motivation and hygiene factors fit into my view that motivation is largely innate and resides in the individual. The manager's job is to encourage the flow of that motivation and to remove any obstacles that may impede it. Thus the manager needs to minimise the hygiene factors that cause blockages while building the conditions in which:

> True motivation [can] come from achievement, personal development, job satisfaction and recognition.
>
> **Frederick Herzberg**

ONE LESSON TO TAKE AWAY

The one thing that we can say about motivation with some certainty is that there is considerable variation in what motivates individuals. Therefore, it is vital that you get to know your staff, their likes, dislikes, ambitions, personal circumstances, etc. In other words, you need to know them as individuals.

If you have 200 staff working for you, then it's difficult, if not impossible, to have this level of knowledge. You need team leaders, supervisors, junior managers and others to act on your behalf. So train these key people in what you want them to do and how you expect them to treat staff.

SECTION 6

DECISION MAKING

INTRODUCTION

In management terms, it's decision making that separates those managers who are destined for great things from middle managers. The reason good decision makers are successful senior managers is because they consider problems in their entirety, not just one aspect of them. Too often, managers look at issues from their own professional background. This myopathy reduces their effectiveness as a decision maker and they end up making sub-optimal decisions because of their bias. You need to avoid this trap if you are to progress in your career and/or become a better decision maker.

This section is even more wide-ranging than that on motivation, with no two entries sharing any significant overlap. The nearest we have to an overlap is between Quotations 51 and 54. However, the difference between these is still significant. Ken Blanchard suggests that decisions should be made by staff while Rosabeth Moss Kanter suggests that managers use information gathered from front-line staff.

We all have our own decision-making approach; as you read this section, try to identify one or two ideas that you can integrate easily into your own approach. If they bear fruit, come back and try another idea. Don't try and revolutionise your approach overnight. That's a high-risk strategy. Aim for evolution, not revolution.

QUOTATION 49 # ROBERT TOWNSEND ON KEEPING DECISIONS SIMPLE

Use this as a guide to making all decisions.

Robert Townsend (1920–98) was CEO of Avis Rent a Car and writer of the bestselling management book of the 1970s, *Up the Organisation.* He believed that work should be fun and if you weren't enjoying it you should get out and do something you did enjoy.

There was very little management theory in what he wrote. What he had to say was based on his experience of turning Avis from a basket case into the second biggest player in the American car rental business.

> There are only two types of decisions, those that are expensive to change and those that are not.
>
> **Robert Townsend**

Not everyone is a good decision maker. Some spend an age collecting data and worrying over every little detail. Others barely look at the data and seem to make instantaneous decisions, which to onlookers can appear cavalier and overly risky. Interestingly, there is no research evidence to show which style of decision making is the most effective. This may have something to do with the fact that decisions are about the future and no one can do that accurately. Luck plays a significant part in every decision.

WHAT TO DO

- Have the confidence to take decisions that are cheap and easy to correct quickly with minimal information. The cost of collecting additional information may well be more than getting the decisions wrong. In addition, such prevarication may lead to delays in taking a more important decision.
- Remember, failure to take 'cheap decisions' quickly will get you a reputation for being indecisive.
- Delay taking decisions that are expensive and difficult to correct until you have adequate, but not complete, data. What constitutes adequate data will depend on the nature of the decision and how

much uncertainty you can live with. What you must not do is use the collection of further data as an excuse for delaying your decision.

- While you can never have complete data when making a decision (if you did there would be no decision to be made), you should subject the data you do have to critical evaluation. Ask yourself to what extent the data has been affected by: incorrect assumptions, wishful thinking, errors in calculation, over-optimistic projections, including customer numbers and cash flows or an underestimation of risk.

- It's worth remembering when looking at future projections that accountants are trained to be pessimistic/prudent in their forecasts, whereas sales people are, by training and group culture, overly optimistic.

- Always carry out a post-decision review. If you don't, you're missing a great opportunity to identify weaknesses and strengths in your decision-making process, both of which can improve future performance (see Quotation 69).

QUESTIONS TO ASK

- What level of data do I require before I make a decision?
- Do I need to vary the amount of data I require between cheap and expensive decisions?

QUOTATION 50 | # HELGA DRUMMOND ON WHY YOU SHOULD NEVER CHASE YOUR LOSSES

Use this as your second principle of decision making.

Helga Drummond is Professor of Decision Sciences at the University of Liverpool Management School and has written widely on decision making, including *The Economist Guide to Decision-making: Getting it more right than wrong.*

She argues that one of the major mistakes made by decision makers is is not knowing when to cut their losses:

> Making a wrong decision is bad enough, throwing good money after bad by persisting with the wrong course of action is worse.
>
> **Helga Drummond**

WHAT TO DO

- The above is a simple maxim and its meaning is immediately clear. However, it can prove extremely difficult to apply in the real world because of the decision maker's ego. When that happens, their pride gets in the way of analytical thought, and they seek to maintain or recover their reputation by throwing good money after bad in the hope that everything will be all right in the end. Don't let your ego rule your head.

- Never take into account what has already been spent when making a decision. That money is gone, whatever you decide. Yes, it's embarrassing to lose £10m on a project, but it's even more embarrassing if you try to save a failing project and spend a further £20m in the process. Only take into account future cash flows when making your decision. For example, if you have already spent £3m on a project and need to spend a further £4m to complete it, compare that additional £4m with future cash flows, not £7m (£3m + £4m). If future receipts are predicted to exceed £4m, you might decide to proceed but if they are below that figure you fold.

- Never think, 'Gosh, we've spent a fortune on this project, we've got to get something for the money we've already spent.' Such thinking is the decision maker attempting to salvage their reputation by trying to deliver something, anything, for the money already spent. It's stupid. Avoid it.
- Competitive, egotistical and obsessed people are the ones most likely to chase their losses. They can't stand the thought that they may have been wrong and that now their colleagues and others will see that they were wrong. Don't let what other people think of you drive your decision making. Know when to fold.

QUESTIONS TO ASK

- Have I ever chased my losses on a decision of mine? Why did I do it?
- Do I become emotionally involved in the decisions I take or do I remain detached?

QUOTATION 51

KENNETH BLANCHARD ON DELEGATING DECISIONS TO FRONT-LINE STAFF

Use this to remind you that front-line staff may be in a position to make better decisions than you.

Kenneth Blanchard (b. 1939) is a management expert and writer, famous for his work on the *One Minute Manager* series of books. He also has an interest in decision making and advocates pushing the responsibility for making business decisions down to the lowest possible level:

> If you want people on the front lines . . . to be responsible for making decisions they must be given the same information that managers use to make good business decisions.
>
> **Kenneth Blanchard**

I fully agree with the sentiments behind the above quotation. However, I disagree with the idea that front-line staff should have the **same** information as managers. Managers work off summarised information and, the more senior the manager, the shorter the briefing note. This is because senior managers have to deal with issues from across the organisation and can't spend time reading detailed reports on, say, the problems with packaging. On the other hand, the manager of the packing department is likely to have a great deal of detailed information about what the problem is and possible solutions. In effect, the packing manager has richer information than any senior manager. If they don't, they aren't doing their job.

WHAT TO DO

- Always delegate decisions down to the lowest possible level in the organisation, be that a manager, supervisor or individual member of staff. Sometimes, decisions are too important or complex to delegate, but the Pareto Principle (see Quotation 55) tells us that over 80 per cent can be safely delegated.
- Inform everyone who has the power to make a decision of the limits of their discretion. For example, the packaging manager can make all

decisions under £44,999; decisions between £50,000 and £149,999 will need to be countersigned by the packing manager's boss; and decisions over £150,000 must be referred to X along with the packaging manager's recommendation for approval.

■ Do a training needs analysis (see Quotation 15) and provide training for any manager whose knowledge of decision-making techniques is weak, e.g. poor understanding of discounted cash flow.

■ In conjunction with each decision maker, identify what regular reports they need from finance, production, sales, etc. in order to do their job. Also make clear to those who produce these reports that they may be required by managers to turn out ad hoc reports when required. Such requests are to be treated as important and not left on the back burner.

■ No one should be hung out to dry for making a bad decision. Robert Townsend (Quotation 49) said that a good manager gets 33 per cent of decisions right, 33 per cent wrong and for the rest it doesn't matter what you decided; things would have turned out just the same. So we all make mistakes and, with luck, learn from them. If you castigate staff for making an honest mistake, word will quickly get round and staff will start referring decisions up the line.

QUESTIONS TO ASK

■ Do I worry about delegating decisions to staff?
■ Do I dump work on staff rather than delegate it?

QUOTATION 52   # BUD HADFIELD ON THE VALUE OF GUT INSTINCT IN DECISION MAKING

Use this to justify your use of gut instinct.

Bud Hadfield (1923–2011) was the entrepreneur who founded Kwik Kopy in the United States. A hugely successful businessman and writer, he recognised that not all data can be quantified.

> When it's time to make a decision about a person or a problem . . . trust your intuition [and] act.
>
> **Bud Hadfield**

Bud Hadfield is not alone in thinking that managers should rely more on their gut instinct. Friedrich von Hayek won the Nobel Prize for Economics for his work on free markets. He showed that one of the reasons why planned economies are always doomed to fail is that it is impossible for decentralised staff to report everything they know about local conditions, problems and opportunities to the centre. This is because much of their knowledge resides in their subconscious but informs their thinking and actions on a daily basis without them being aware of it.

You have probably encountered numerous situations where you 'just knew' what the right decision was and were subsequently proved correct. Or maybe you've been on the end of a new manager's decision to implement a new policy or process that you and your staff know is doomed to failure but can't put forward a reasoned argument as to why it will fail. Which of course it subsequently does and the manager blames the staff's lack of support for the failure. In both cases, it was your tacit knowledge at work.

So how can you improve your tacit knowledge?

WHAT TO DO

- The key to increasing tacit knowledge is to store information in your mind. Use every opportunity to gather information about your organisation from staff, managers, customers, suppliers and wider stakeholders constantly.

- Walk the job (see Quotation 54) and talk to everyone, from the office cleaner (you'd be amazed at what information they see lying around on people's desks) to senior executives and members of the board and everyone in between.

- Use meetings and the general chats and banter that occurs before and after them as an opportunity to add to your store of information.

- Use observation at meetings to learn about the people present, including their attitudes, beliefs, motives and relationship with colleagues.

- Read reports that appear in the press or on the web about your organisation.

- Always be on the lookout for clever ideas in other organisations and sectors that you can import and adapt for use in yours (see Quotation 82).

- Keep a learning journal and jot down any interesting comments, events, trends, problems, opportunities, threats or juicy gossip that has any bearing on your company.

- Even stuff you see on TV or come across in books, newspapers and professional journals can be useful fodder for your tacit knowledge.

- Your unconscious mind accumulates all these disparate and unconnected pieces of data where they are allowed to 'compost down' and form linkages and connections in your brain which enrich your tacit knowledge. Then, when faced with a problem, this knowledge will inform your thinking either consciously or subconsciously and provide you with an answer.

QUESTIONS TO ASK

- Do I use a mixture of hard data and instinct when making decisions?
- Do I try and exclude what my gut is telling me when I make a decision?

QUOTATION 53 # MARY PARKER FOLLETT ON WHY THERE ARE ALWAYS MORE THAN TWO CHOICES (TOP TEN ENTRY)

Use this to remind you that there is always an alternative course of action – you just haven't thought of it yet.

Mary Parker Follet (1868–1933) was an American social worker, management consultant and pioneer of organisational theory at a time when there were very few women in the field of management studies.

> We should never allow ourselves to be bullied by an either-or. There is often the possibility of something better than either of these two alternatives.
>
> **Mary Parker Follett**

Among her many accomplishments, Mary Parker Follett was also a philosopher. It's perhaps for that reason that she refused to believe that in the social world any decision could come down to just two alternatives.

WHAT TO DO

- As a manager you are often asked to make a decision based upon two alternatives. Staff presenting the data to you do this either to make the decision easier and quicker for you or because they have a preference and they have slanted their report/presentation in that direction.
- If the decision is cheap and easy to correct if it goes wrong, follow Townsend's advice (see Quotation 49) and choose between the two options on offer.
- If the decision involves a large investment in time and money, you should ask about the alternative options that were considered and rejected. It is entirely possible that, because you know more about the organisation than those reporting to you, you will see advantages in a proposal that they rejected. In addition, as you discuss the alternatives, you may identify other courses of action you could adopt, perhaps by combining elements of two or more ideas.

- If you are responsible for submitting suggestions, by all means present the best one or two alternatives, but be prepared to outline succinctly the other courses of action that could be adopted or include a précis of them as an appendix.

- When making a decision, avoid tramline thinking which leads you to think in terms of an either-or solution. One way to do this is to work with a small team of people. Present the problem and the information you have to them and ask them to suggest suitable approaches. Then withdraw and leave them to it. What you are looking for are fresh ideas and perspectives, so don't share with them your preferred option until after they have reported their findings.

QUESTIONS TO ASK

- How wide do I spread my net when thinking about alternative approaches to a problem?
- Do I generally only see one or two possible answers and then plough ahead evaluating those to the exclusion of other possibilities?

ROSABETH MOSS KANTER ON WHY THE BEST INFORMATION DOES NOT RESIDE IN EXECUTIVE OFFICES

Use this to encourage you to get out of the office and talk to people.

Rosabeth Moss Kanter (b. 1943) is a professor of business at the Harvard Business School, an expert in change management and a highly successful writer on management. She is a supporter of management by walking about (MBWA) as a means by which executives can keep in touch with what is happening on the shop floor.

> People who are making decisions about the future often don't have access to some of the best ideas in the company, which may be at the periphery or at lower levels [of the organisation].
>
> **Rosabeth Moss Kanter**

WHAT TO DO

- Schedule time every week to get out of your office and undertake a bit of management by walking about (MBWA). How long you spend on your walk will depend on your seniority. Junior and middle managers are near the front line and usually have a good knowledge of what's going on. Senior managers, executives and board members are usually too remote to know. It's the latter group that needs to indulge in MBWA.

- Vary the day, time and locations you visit, otherwise people will prepare for the visit, which is not what you want. You want an informal chat with staff, not a scheduled meeting.

- For every walk, identify a purpose, e.g. how do staff feel about the latest restructuring? However, be prepared to change it if someone raises an issue with you. Your aim is to listen to the staff's view and concerns and not collect data on the concerns you think they should have.

- Your overall aim is always the same: to discover what people feel and think about what's going on in the organisation and how it has affected their relationships with other staff, departments, suppliers, customers and other stakeholders.

- Listen to what people say. Don't tell them what you think. Use your eyes to see how different sections, teams and departments behave and interact. Keep your mouth shut and your ears open.

- Hold meetings sparingly but, when you do, use them to deal with the issues under consideration and as an opportunity to collect other information also, e.g. which people/departments have formed alliances and why? Which manager is at war with a colleague and why? Who is listened to in the meeting and who is ignored? Where does the power reside in the room?

- When talking with staff and other managers informally, listen to what they say. Don't sit there only half listening, planning your wonderful response to what's been said. You learn nothing new when you are doing the talking.

- As you wander around, either make a mental note or jot down anything that strikes you as interesting, unusual, good, bad, worthy of further investigation or strange practices (both good and bad) that you come across.

- Keep a note of the really important stuff that you hear and see and work it into your list of targets and objectives (see Quotation 68).

- Watch Clint Eastwood's hugely entertaining movie *Trouble with the Curve* to see the value of listening to front-line staff.

QUESTIONS TO ASK

- When was the last time that I walked the job?
- How do I know what junior managers, supervisors and staff are thinking and doing?

WARREN BENNIS ON THE VITAL DIFFERENCE BETWEEN INFORMATION AND MEANING

Use this as a reminder to check that you have understood/interpreted the information you have correctly.

Warren Bennis (1925–2014) was an academic, management consultant and writer. He recognised that in today's world leaders have access to an enormous amount of information when they are faced with making a decision. Indeed, the sheer volume of information available can cloud rather than enhance the decision-making process. He observed that:

> There is a profound difference between information and meaning.
>
> **Warren Bennis**

A good example of the difference between information and meaning is provided by newly diagnosed cancer sufferers. In recent research, over 30 per cent of patients who were awaiting confirmation of diagnosis thought that a positive result meant they were free of cancer. They had the information but misunderstood its meaning.

WHAT TO DO

- First you need to identify what information you intend to take account of in your deliberations. To help you do that use Vilfredo Pareto's famous theory (the Pareto Principle) that, in any situation, 20 per cent of the population in question will contain 80 per cent of the value. In this case, 20 per cent of the data you have will contain 80 per cent of the information you need to make your decision.
- Use your experience of the organisation, the market you operate and past decisions to identify what information is important.
- The Pareto Principle doesn't solve your problem. Rather it provides a tool to save time and point you towards where the most effective action can be taken. If you have an issue, always start by identifying the vital few.

■ Concentrate your attention on this 20 per cent of information. Seek to understand it fully. Find the people who produced the information and ask them what it actually means. For example, many managers I've worked with have made decisions based on financial information that they didn't fully understand. But they were too embarrassed to ask for clarification because they didn't want to appear stupid.

■ Check to see whether the information is pessimistic (often the case with accounting projections) or overly optimistic (regularly the case with sales managers' forecasts).

■ Be willing to collect vital information from those who know what's really going on, i.e. the front-line staff (see Quotation 54).

QUESTIONS TO ASK

■ Who do I rely upon for supplying me with decision-making information? How good has the information been?

■ What other sources of information should I regularly access when making a decision?

PETER DRUCKER AND THE POWER TO SAY NO

Use this to remind you that the best decision makers know when to say no.

Peter Drucker (1909–2005), the godfather of management studies, argued strongly that the most important ability of any decision makers was to:

Learn to say no.

Peter Drucker

The ability to say no stood Warren Buffet, the world's most successful investor, in good stead in 1998/9 when he refused to invest in technology stocks and again in 2006/7 when he said no to investing in sub-prime mortgages. In both instances, he justified his decision by saying, 'I don't understand them.' He's not known as the Sage of Omaha for nothing.

Learn to say NO!

NO coming from loud hailer

WHAT TO DO

- As a manager and decision maker, your job isn't to please people. It's to do whatever is best for the organisation. That means you may have to disappoint staff, colleagues and even your boss or board. To do this you have be assertive. That means being able to explain clearly your reasons for saying no and then sticking to them. If you are overruled by your boss or board, then it's their decision not yours and they have to take responsibility for it.
- If you feel that you aren't assertive enough, get some training. A one- or two-day training session will be all you need. It will teach you the basic techniques. It will then be up to you to put them into practice.

The more you practise, the better you'll get at saying no and the easier it will become.

■ Saying no is a particular problem for many inexperienced managers who may lack self-confidence and still feel the need to please people (see Quotation 14). Yet it is precisely when you start to say no that you become a manager and are recognised as such.

■ If you are in an argument about a particular decision with colleagues and all your arguments are based on your professional background knowledge and experience, your opponents will undermine you by saying that you can't see the bigger picture. You must rise above the constraints imposed on you by professional socialisation and see problems in organisational terms. That means understanding all the issues involved in the decision. But, by itself, that's not enough. You have to be willing and able to argue your case and stand toe to toe with those senior to you. Often, that will involve you saying 'No. That's not the right thing to do and these are the reasons why . . . '

QUESTIONS TO ASK

■ How often have I said no to someone's request in the last week?

■ Do I ever say no to my boss or other managers more senior than me?

CONCLUSION

I was never a fan of Prime Minister Margaret Thatcher. One of the reasons that irked me was her constant repetition of the phrase, 'There is no alternative.' This was guaranteed to set my teeth on edge because I firmly believe that in the world of politics and management there is always an alternative and I distrust anyone who claims that there isn't. That's why I had to choose Mary Parker Follett's quotation as a member of the Top Ten:

> We should never allow ourselves to be bullied by an either-or. There is often the possibility of something better than either of these two alternatives.
>
> **Mary Parker Follett**

ONE LESSON TO TAKE AWAY

As a manager, whenever you are presented with a binary decision, remember that you have the right to reject both options and seek an alternative. While you are checking out the options available, remember the difference between information and meaning. Never make a decision based upon information. Instead, base all decisions on what the information actually means in the real world (see Quotation 55). Okay, so that's two lessons I want you to take from this section. So what? It's Sunday and I'm running a special 2-for-1 offer and I was an accountant so I can make 1 + 1 = 1.

SECTION 7

CHANGE MANAGEMENT

INTRODUCTION

Change is a risky business. It's a step into the unknown and that involves risk. Niccolò Machiavelli obviously understood what was involved when any leader decided to implement a significant change, namely:

> There is nothing more difficult to take in hand, more perilous to conduct, or more uncertain in its success, than to take the lead in the introduction of a new order of things.
>
> **Niccolò Machiavelli**

Of course you can always refuse to change but, as evolution has taught us, that way leads to extinction.

This section contains range of ideas. Quotation/s:

- 57 argues that the best changes are those that are made from the bottom up.
- 58 and 59 offer a warning about the dangers of change overload and the need to maintain some sense of continuity for the benefit of staff.
- 60 and 61 deal with the danger points in any change process.
- 62 and 63 offer competing advice. Quotation 62 suggests that you should always make the change before you have to, but quotation 63 suggests that there is one area of change that you should avoid for as long as possible, namely organisational culture.

As you read the entries in this section you will quickly realise that all the commentators share one objective: that is to minimise the risks associated with change. This is an area to which many project managers pay insufficient attention during their project planning.

Please note: While I recognise that not every change is a project, many significant changes are run as a project. Therefore, I've used the words 'change' and 'project' interchangeably in this section.

GARY HAMEL ON WHY CHANGE SHOULD BE FROM THE BOTTOM UP

Use this to remind you that front-line staff are a vital source of ideas and information.

Gary P. Hamel (b. 1954) is an American academic, management consultant and founder of Strategos, an international management consulting firm based in Chicago. He has written extensively on a range of management issues, including change management. Like Tom Peters and others, he laments the lack of use that managers make of the knowledge and skills of front-line staff:

> This extraordinary arrogance that change must start at the top is a way of guaranteeing that change will not happen in most organisations.
>
> **Gary P. Hamel**

The major reason that change fails is that in many organisations management decide on a change, call together a small team to plan and implement the change and, when they are ready to roll it out, they expect staff to implement it without question. They seem to believe that their every whim, idea and detail will be implemented without any trouble. What delusional rubbish.

WHAT TO DO

- Recognise that staff are intelligent adults with a great deal of expert knowledge about the job they do. They have the detail about the firm's operations that few, if any, manager has and certainly more than any business or IT consultant will ever discover through research (see Quotation 84). You would be mad not to use that expertise when planning a change.
- Encourage staff to come forward with ideas for how to improve the organisational performance. Don't limit staff to just making recommendations about their team or section. If someone makes a suggestion that requires additional work, invite the person to work up the idea with you and, when you present it to management,

recognise the part they played in it. Reward them for their efforts (see Quotation 45).

■ Use management by walking about as an opportunity to pick up suggestions for improvements from staff (see Quotation 54).

■ If the change idea originates from the top, insist on having representatives of those staff who are most directly affected by the change on your planning and implementation team. Use their expert knowledge to identify what's feasible, potential bottlenecks and the likely reaction to the changes from staff and junior managers.

■ Train a selection of front-line staff to act as change agents and change champions. An agent is always on the look-out for possible ways to improve processes, procedures and services. Champions act as cheer leaders for the change before and during the implementation phase of the project. Often the same person will be both an agent and champion. Change agents and champions work side by side with staff on a daily basis. This gives them a credibility that few managers can ever achieve. It also enables them to squash rumours at birth, act as a two-way channel of communication between staff and management and identify problems early and warn management of potential problems.

QUESTIONS TO ASK

■ How much credence do I give to the ideas of junior staff? Do I ignore them or try to show why they won't work or do I work with the person to see whether it has legs?

■ To what extent do I announce decisions and expect staff to implement them without question?

QUOTATION 58   # MICHAEL HAMMER AND JAMES CHAMPY ON WHY TOO MUCH CHANGE CAN KILL AN ORGANISATION

Use this as a reality check as to how much change you and your staff can handle.

Michael Hammer and James Champy, authors of *Re-engineering the Corporation: A Manifesto for Business Revolution* (2004) suggest that:

> An organisation becomes bewildered rather than energised when it's asked to do too much at once.
>
> **Michael Hammer and James Champy**

The change management business really got underway during the 1990s and remains with us today. Unfortunately, many changes are implemented not because they are required but because the manager wants to be seen doing something or to enhance their CV (see Quotation 11).

WHAT TO DO

■ Never be afraid to implement changes when they are required. Your loyalty should be to the organisation and it's your duty to act in its best interests. If that means making unpopular changes, so be it.

■ Like a doctor, analyse what the problem is or is going to be and treat that and only that. If a patient visits the doctor with a wound to their forearm, the doctor knows that, left untreated, the person could die. But they don't amputate the whole arm. They treat the wound and stop infection spreading. Too many managers amputate the entire arm as a first option. They throw out both the good and bad practices/systems/procedures and replace them with an untried new approach. This is a risky business, makes the change more difficult to implement and annoys the staff involved because they are the ones that will have to implement and live with the unnecessary changes.

■ Recognise that, based upon past experiences, people have different change-level tolerances. Even minor changes for some are traumatic and render them unable to think or act effectively. Others will see change as a great adventure and, like an adrenalin junkie, will always want more. Many managers fall into this latter category.

■ You must win over those who fear change. The only way you can do this is through constant communication and reassurance. During any change you should be both accessible and visible to all staff. Emphasise to managers, supervisors and those you have identified as change champions (see Quotation 57) about the need to 'hold the hand of those who are fearful'.

■ If a major change is to be implemented, break it down into a series of stages. Treat each stage as a mini project. Celebrate the successful implementation of each stage before you move on to the next. This approach builds confidence, reassures the fearful and minimises change fatigue in the staff.

■ You might also consider using the Pareto Principle (see Quotations 15 and 55). Most of the benefits from any change can be achieved by implementing the 80 per cent of the project that takes up only 20 per cent of the time. This approach is ideal as a way of building support for the project. People will see significant progress in a very short time. Then, with the pressure off, you can tackle the troublesome 20 per cent of the project that will tie you up for 80 per cent of the time.

QUESTIONS TO ASK

■ Do I enjoy change or do I worry about it?
■ Do I know how my staff feel about change?

QUOTATION 59 PETER DRUCKER ON THE NEED FOR CONTINUITY IN A PERIOD OF CHANGE

Use this as the basis for your plan to reassure staff during a period of change.

Peter Drucker (1909–2005), the most influential of all management writers, was interested in all aspects of management, including change management. With his usual insight, he identified that, in many organisations, there is a disjunction between the organisation's change agenda and people's need for continuity and consistency, namely:

> Organisations that are change leaders are designed for change. But people need continuity . . . they do not function well if the environment is not predictable, not understandable, not known.
>
> **Peter Drucker**

WHAT TO DO

- In any change situation, staff need to be reassured that after the upheaval they will still have a job and a future. As manager, you are responsible for providing that reassurance.
- Aim to give staff as much information as possible about how the change will affect them and their work and what training they will be given to help them adjust to the new environment.
- Provide all staff with the training they need to operate effectively in the post-change world. Knowing that they will be able to cope will reduce the levels of stress that staff feel. This means that they will be more willing to listen to you and others during the transition and are less likely to be seduced by claims that 'We're all doomed.'
- Involve staff in the design of the change as early as possible. This will give them some reassurance that they have at least a modicum of control over events and that their voice is being listened to. It will also build trust between you and the staff so that, down the line, when you speak to them they are more likely to believe you.

- Regular and continuous communication between you and staff is vital. Encourage staff to discuss their fears and concerns. Use every means you can to get your message and reassurances across, including formal and informal meetings, email, newsletters, casual conversations and management by walking about (MBWA) (see Quotation 54). Use these walks to discover what staff really think and feel about the change. Always answer people's questions as fully as possible. If you can't answer a question, say so and promise to get them an answer within the next 24 hours.

- Never try to bamboozle people with management speak or technical jargon. Talk to them in plain, clear, simple English and always deliver on any promises you make.

- Appoint change champions from front-line staff (see Quotation 57). One of their key tasks will be to show staff how, despite the changes, there will still be a role for them after the change and that, although relationships with colleagues and managers may alter, they will not disappear.

QUESTIONS TO ASK

- How good am I at involving staff in planning and decision making?
- Do staff think that I'm approachable or stand-offish?

QUOTATION 60

DANIEL WEBSTER ON WHY IT'S NOT THE CHANGE THAT KILLS YOU, IT'S THE TRANSITION

Use this to prepare yourself for the inevitable dip in enthusiasm and belief that occurs during any change project.

Daniel Webster (1782–1852) was a leading American senator and statesman during the 1830s and 40s. This was a period of uncertainty and upheaval and this may have prompted him to observe that:

> It isn't the changes that do you in, it's the transition.
>
> **Daniel Webster**

Webster was talking about the dangers of rolling out the change once a decision has been made. The implementation of any change is only complete when people stop looking back at what they used to do and accept the changed world they work in as the new norm.

WHAT TO DO

- Accept that in every change the transition phase between implementation and full acceptance of the new order is fraught with problems and plan for it.
- It's easy to become despondent when you run into transitional problems. After all, you've been working like a galley slave to implement the change and now that it's here people are still resisting it. Don't let it get you down. It's all part of the process. The problem is not unique to you. Expect it and plan for it.
- Ensure that all the required training is delivered to staff prior to implementation of the change.
- Use your change agents/champions to identify problems and deal with those they can and report the remainder to you immediately.
- Walk the job and be seen by the staff affected by the change. Give them an opportunity to ask questions and let off steam. Make a note

of any issue that you can't deal with immediately and promise to look into it and get back to the staff concerned. Then do just that.

■ Analyse the feedback you have received from the change agents/ champions, managers, supervisors and your own findings from walking the job and identify problems and trends.

■ You will be able to analyse most of the problems under three categories:

– Poor communication between management and staff. Find the breakdown or bottleneck and deal with it. You and your managers, supervisors and change agents/champions must give communication with staff the highest priority during the transition stage.

– Poor training, gaps in the training provided to people forgetting what they were taught or issues arising in practice that were not foreseen are all problems you will have to deal with. Arrange to provide follow-up training to deal with all the issues identified.

– Unforeseen problems with the change. These can range in scope from disastrous to minor irritants. One of the most disastrous changes made by a company in recent times was Coca-Cola's decision to change the taste of America's favourite drink. However, they rescued the decision by quickly recognising their error and reverting to the old formula. That's what you have to do: act quickly to correct minor and major issues associated with the change. For that reason, never disband any project team you have created until the change has been fully implemented.

QUESTIONS TO ASK

■ Do I plan for the difficulties that inevitably arise during every transition stage?

■ How am I going to monitor the staff's morale during the dangerous transition stage?

QUOTATION 61 # NICCOLÒ MACHIAVELLI ON THE ENEMIES OF CHANGE (TOP TEN ENTRY)

Use this to identify those who can disrupt your change mid-stream.

Niccolò Machiavelli (1469–1527), diplomat, statesman, political philosopher and writer, continues to influence all those interested in power and influence. He summed up the problems faced by anyone who wants to implement a change as follows:

> The reformer has enemies in all who profit by the old order, and only lukewarm defenders in those who would profit by the new order.
>
> **Niccolò Machiavelli**

Identifying these enemies and their potential strength is the first step in defending yourself against their attacks.

WHAT TO DO

- Use Gerry Johnson, Kevin Scholes and Richard Wittingham's model to map both the enemies of change and possible allies that may be able to help you.

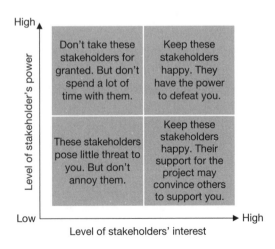

- Identify as many stakeholders as you can and plot their position on the figure shown. You are most interested in the people who have high power and high interest in the change.

- Once the potential key players have been identified, make yourself known to them and seek to win their confidence. Talk to them and try to discover how they feel about you and the proposed change.

- If possible, get them to commit their support to you and your change. If they are unwilling to commit themselves one way or the other, find out what's likely to motivate them to either support or oppose you. Use this information to design a strategy that will win their support and/or minimise their opposition.

- Monitor the actions and statements of those stakeholders who have low interest and low power. But don't invest too much time and effort in them.

- Canvass those with little power but high interest. They are the ones who probably know most about the change. This expert power (see Quotation 71) may prove very valuable when it comes to convincing more powerful stakeholders to back you.

- Keep those with high power and little interest happy, content and on the side lines. Don't do anything that will upset them and cause them to come in against you. Find out what red lines they have and don't cross them.

- Obviously, most of your efforts should be directed towards those stakeholders with high power and high interest. These are the people you need to fully engage with if you are to get the job done.

- If you can't convince someone with high power and interest to back you, find someone in your camp who has influence with the person (see Quotation 72) and ask them to speak to them. It shouldn't be the case, but sometimes it's not the message that people dislike, it's the messenger.

QUESTIONS TO ASK

- How much attention do I pay to consideration of the stakeholders' interests when making a decision?

- Which stakeholders have I upset in the past? What can I do to mend fences?

QUOTATION 62 # SETH GODIN ON THE NEED TO MAKE CHANGES BEFORE YOU'RE FORCED TO

Use this to remind you not to delay making changes when they are required.

Seth Godin (b. 1960), American entrepreneur, author and public speaker recognises that, as with any decision, the timing of when to embark on a change project is vital. There is never a good time to implement a major change; inevitably, it will cause disruption, additional work, concern among staff and possibly a temporary dip in productivity. However, any delay can be disastrous because:

> Change almost never fails because it is too early. It almost always fails because it was too late.
>
> **Seth Godin**

It is often said that people only change when the pain of staying the same becomes greater than the pain caused by changing. Certainly there is evidence that many people are change averse and would like nothing better than to carry on as they are. Unfortunately, if a business has the same mentality, then they will be quickly overtaken by competitors and soon find themselves out of business.

As US General Eric Shinseki, Chief of Staff, US Army said, 'If you don' like change you're going to like irrelevance even less.'

WHAT TO DO

- Every change starts with a decision. Use the advice provided by Robert Townsend (see Quotation 49) and take low-cost, easy-to-change decisions quickly. For more costly decisions, identify and collect the essential data that you need to make an effective decision (see Quotation 54).
- Avoid becoming a victim to paralysis by analysis, always wanting more information before you make a decision. Recognise that you

can never have perfect information and that, after a certain point, the law of diminishing returns sets in.

■ Use the Pareto Principle (see Quotation 55) and collect the 80 per cent of the data that is readily available and takes only 20 per cent of the time/effort to collect. Base your decision on this information. The remaining 20 per cent is likely be of marginal use.

■ Once the decision has been made to implement a change, accelerate into the next stage. Pull together a small working team, including some change agents/change champions (see Quotation 57) from the front-line staff, and plan the change.

■ Identify the aims, objectives and milestones for the change project and use those to monitor progress. Hold weekly project team meetings and monthly meetings with the project sponsors. There are only two topics of conversation for each meeting: (i) progress to date against target and (ii) cost to date against budget. Avoid adding any additional meetings. They take staff away from the important work.

■ Resist changing the content of the project. Only accept essential additions.

■ As the project is being developed, train staff to deal with the revised policies, procedures or practices. This will reduce their concerns about the change and ease the eventual implementation.

■ Implement the change and ensure that every member of the project team is available to deal with queries and concerns from staff.

■ Evaluate the impact of the change and determine to what extent it has addressed the reasons change was required. If some concerns have not been met, address them as a matter of urgency.

QUESTIONS TO ASK

■ What early warning systems do I have in place to tell me that a change is required?

■ Do I personally resist change?

QUOTATION 63   # PETER DRUCKER ON WHY CHANGING AN ORGANISATION'S CULTURE SHOULD BE AVOIDED

Use this as a reminder of how difficult and dangerous it is to change an organisation's culture.

Peter Drucker (1909–2005) was hugely successful as a management thinker and writer. One reason for this was his down-to-earth practical approach which chimed well with busy managers in every type of organisation. On the question of organisational cultures, he suggested that:

> Company cultures are like country cultures. Never try to change one. Try instead to work with what you've got.
>
> **Peter Drucker**

Many writers have argued that the role of a leader is to change an organisation's culture while that of the manager is to spread and uphold the organisational culture. Drucker warns us that you mess with organisational cultures at your peril.

WHAT TO DO

- It is not uncommon to read in the business press that a new chief executive or chairperson has been appointed by Any Company Ltd with a remit to change its organisational culture. It happened to a lot in banks after the 2008 financial crisis. Unfortunately, Drucker believes that this is a near impossible task, which will require a huge commitment in terms of time, money and effort by all connected with the organisation and, on balance, should be avoided, if possible.

- Despite Drucker's warnings, many newly appointed chief executives or chairpersons will decimate the senior management team on appointment and bring in their own tried and trusted people to run the organisation. Claims will then be made that this has resulted in a cultural change in the organisation. This is seldom the case. Organisational culture is multifaceted and is not easily destroyed or changed, as it consists of the basic assumptions, beliefs, expectations, norms and values that are shared by the staff within the organisation. These assumptions have been influenced by the organisation's myths, history, rituals, routines, structure, purpose and traditions.

■ Only if the organisation is in desperate need of a new culture should you attempt to change it. Changing a few of the top managers isn't going to make much of a dent on the above factors and certainly not in the short term. If you want genuine change, you have to accept it's a long-term project, not the work of a single month or year but one that is likely to engage you over several years. Think carefully before you commit yourself to this task as it will occupy a huge amount of your time.

■ If the risk of undertaking a total overhaul is too great, think about making incremental changes. For example, the appointment of more women, ethnic minorities and those with disabilities to management posts will get the ball rolling and open the way to new ideas and approaches.

QUESTIONS TO ASK

■ Are there any aspects of the organisation's culture that I think require changing? If so, what can I do about it?

■ Do I find it easy to live with the organisation's culture? If not, should I move jobs?

CONCLUSION

I have a soft spot for Machiavelli. He wrote *The Prince* as a job application and, while every democratically elected politician pretends that he hasn't studied the master's work, you can be damn sure that they have. The reason he's so popular is that he is remarkably accurate when it comes to explaining how people think and act. For that reason I selected him as a Top Ten entry. He is also a brilliant writer, able to sum up attitudes and issues in just a few words, as shown by his quotation on change:

> The reformer has enemies in all who profit by the old order, and only lukewarm defenders in those who would profit by the new order.
>
> **Niccolò Machiavelli**

ONE LESSON TO TAKE AWAY

All change involves risk and, while you should always expect and work for success, you must also plan for opposition and obstructions. Do that and you will dramatically improve your chances of success.

SECTION 8

PLANNING

INTRODUCTION

P lanning requires you to predict the future and no one can predict the future unless they have a DeLorean time machine built by Doc Brown sitting in their garage. That's why Malcolm Forbes said:

> Anyone who says a businessman deals in facts, not fiction, has never read five-year-old projections.
>
> **Malcolm Forbes**

Five out of the six quotations in this section deal with different aspects of uncertainty in the planning process while the sixth offers advice on how to improve future planning effectiveness. Thus, Quotation/s:

- 64 suggests that the benefits of planning lie in the knowledge gained during the planning process rather than the actual plan itself, which often proves to be inaccurate in its forecasts and assumptions.
- 65 to 67 offer ways to either improve the accuracy of the plan or compensate for its inaccuracies.
- 68 emphasises the need to specify clearly the strategic goals of the organisation and to reject suggestions that can obstruct their achievement or confuse staff about their priorities.
- 69 emphasises the value of undertaking a regular evaluation of the organisation's strategy.

While reading this section, try to identify some of the strengths and weaknesses of the approaches that you and your organisation take to planning.

QUOTATION 64 # DWIGHT D. EISENHOWER ON WHY PLANS ARE USELESS BUT PLANNING IS ESSENTIAL

Use this to remind you of the benefits of planning.

General Dwight D. Eisenhower (1890–1969) was Commander-in-Chief of the Allied Forces in Europe during the Second World War and later served as a two-term President of the United States. As the man responsible for overseeing the invasion of Europe, he was intimately involved in the planning that went into D-Day. Despite all that, he famously said:

> In preparing for battle I have always found that plans are useless, but planning is indispensable.
>
> **Dwight D. Eisenhower**

It is often said that truth is the first casualty of war; if that is the case, General Eisenhower is reminding us that the second casualty is planning. Nothing ever goes to plan in a battle or a war. By their nature they are chaotic. However, by planning for as many possibilities as he could, Eisenhower was able to react to changing conditions because he had the information he required to make decisions.

WHAT TO DO

- Recognise and accept that it is impossible to produce the perfect plan. The more chaotic and changeable the environment you are working in, the less accurate your predictions of future conditions will be. Even in relatively benign circumstances one unforeseen event can render your plan totally unworkable/inaccurate.

- Knowing that totally accuracy is impossible don't insist on working everything out to 'three decimal points'. Invest time on drawing up those plans that only extend six to twelve months into the future. After that prepare outline rolling plans that can be updated as you go along. This will save you time and improve the accuracy of your forecasts. That said, there is still no guarantee that they will be 100 per cent accurate.

■ To deal with inaccuracies caused by 'unforeseen events', engage in scenario planning (see Quotation 67). Pull together a small team of people and work with them to identify those factors that could impact on your organisation over the planning period.

■ Analyse and evaluate each scenario on the basis of how likely it is to happen and what the effect will be on the organisation if it does happen. This gives rise to the following table of risk.

- High risk of occurring/low cost
- High risk of occurring/high cost
- Low risk of occurrence/low cost
- Low risk of occurring /high cost

■ Concentrate on developing contingency plans for high risk/high cost and low risk/high cost events. Draw up reasonably detailed plans for dealing with the high risk/high cost eventualities but save the really detailed planning until the likelihood of them occurring becomes more than 50/50. Prepare outline plans for the low risk/high cost possibilities.

■ Your detailed consideration of possible future events and how you might deal with them, should they occur, will enable you to respond more effectively to unforeseen events in the future and to amend your plans as required. It's still not perfect but it's better than facing the future on little more than a wing and a prayer.

QUESTIONS TO ASK

■ What role am I expected to play in the organisation's planning process?

■ Do I draw up a yearly plan for myself and my staff?

ANDREW S. GROVE ON WHY YOU NEED A FLEXIBLE WORKFORCE

Use this to remind you to recruit and train a flexible and responsive workforce.

Andrew S. Grove (1936–2016) was an entrepreneur, author and Chairman of Intel Corp. Recognising that there is much that does remain constant over the short and medium term, he suggested that:

> You need to plan the way a fire department plans: it cannot anticipate where the next fire will be, so it has to shape an energetic and efficient team that is capable of responding to the unanticipated as well as the ordinary event.
>
> **Andrew S. Grove**

WHAT TO DO

- My definition of a good budget is 'a business plan with a price ticket on it.' Everything that an organisation wants to do in the forthcoming year can be reduced to figures and presented in a budget. Now, unless you go out of business, about 80 per cent of an organisation's income and expenditure will remain fairly consistent in the short term – up to one year. For example, one of the largest items of expenditure in an organisation is often salaries and wages. This figure can be calculated very accurately. It's the sort of ordinary events that Grove is referring to.

- The unexpected events are such things as a huge new order arriving out of the blue, a cancellation of a major order, a massive increase in raw material costs. These are events that are difficult to plan for but they are not that unusual and can be taken account of in your plan by using scenario analysis (see Quotation 64).

- Black swan events are the truly exceptional events that cannot be anticipated because they have never happened before, e.g. the 9/11 attacks. Such events will always occur out of the blue. To deal with them you need to:

- Recruit people who are flexible and train existing staff to react quickly to changing events.
- Avoid being shocked into immobility. Start to ask questions and identify the impact that the event may have on you and your organisation immediately. Don't wait for the media analysis – get working.
- While a black swan event can't be predicted, it is valuable to have a group of people who have expertise in planning for major disasters. This group might be the organisation's formal emergency planning team or a small ad hoc group that meets occasionally to imagine the effect of significant unpredicted events on the organisation. The mere fact that they have been trying to identify possible disasters means that they are less likely to be frozen into inaction by the real thing than ordinary staff.

■ When planning, build flexibility into your plans (see Quotation 64). The purpose of a plan is to help you reach your objective. It is not meant to be a strait jacket. When events blow you off course, reassess how you will achieve your objective. Be willing to take detours and back roads but always keep in mind your final destination and try to move towards it.

QUESTIONS TO ASK

■ How flexible am I in my thinking about what might occur in the future?
■ How adaptable am I? How well do I adapt to rapidly changing circumstances?

QUOTATION 66 # EDMUND BURKE ON WHY YOU CAN'T BASE FUTURE PLANS ON PAST EVENTS

Use this to remind you that change is discontinuous.

Edmund Burke (1729–97) was a statesman, author, orator, political theorist and philosopher who, after moving to London, served as a Member of Parliament for many years. He lived through turbulent times and saw both the American and French Revolutions rock the centuries-old certainties and continuing effects of the agrarian revolution change the social fabric of Britain. With the industrial revolution on the horizon, it's hardly surprising that he said:

> You can never plan the future by the past.
>
> **Edmund Burke**

An obvious statement, perhaps. But if you were a particularly bright manager in the late 1950s/60s, you would have been lusting after a job in corporate planning. This was populated by the cadre of managers that organisations expected to fill its executive vacancies. And what did these corporate planners do? They drew up plans for the next 25 years using projections based on the belief that the stability and incremental changes that had characterised 1950s and early 1960s would continue into the future.

All that went out of the window with the oil crisis of 1973 and the cult of the corporate planner disappeared overnight.

WHAT TO DO

- Accept that it's impossible to predict the future and that it can't be extrapolated from past events.
- Recognise that planning now requires you to identify new ideas and trends as they occur, and quickly mobilise the resources you need to capitalise on the opportunity presented or minimise the threat posed.
- Talk to customers, suppliers and competitors to stay abreast of what's 'bubbling under' in the marketplace. In addition, work with

the middle managers and front-line staff in the organisation to identify what customers want, identify current market trends and predict changes. Use this information to produce short-term plans and either anticipate future market trends or react quickly to them when they occur.

■ As unexpected chance events are now the norm, you have to prepare your staff for the constantly changing demands of customers and market circumstances. To do this, staff need to become more flexible and creative when dealing with changing customers' demands and market circumstances. You need to train them in these new soft skills.

■ Instead of drawing up a single plan, write three separate plans based upon the most likely outcome, the worst outcomes and the best.

■ Identify those events, good and bad, that would have significant impact on the organisation and draw up a plan for how you will deal with the opportunity or threat (see Quotations 64 and 65).

QUESTIONS TO ASK

■ Do I have contingency plans for all the significant threats and opportunities that I've identified?

■ Have I trained my staff to cope with sudden and significant change?

QUOTATION 67 # JAMES YORKE ON THE NEED FOR A PLAN B

Use this to remind you that you always need a back-up plan, or two!

James Yorke (b. 1941) was a Professor of Mathematics at the University of Maryland until he retired in 2013. He was awarded the Guggenheim Fellowship for Natural Sciences, US & Canada, in 1980 for his work on chaos theory.

Chaos theory shows how apparently minor events can develop into significant crises. That is why Yorke suggested that:

> The most successful people are those with a plan B.
>
> **James Yorke**

Scenario analysis can improve the planning process by identifying the effect that key variables may have on the organisation in the short and medium term and developing a series of strategies to deal with them should they occur.

WHAT TO DO

- Appoint an experienced external facilitator to help you run the scenario workshops. It is essential that they be willing to challenge the pre-conceived ideas that you and your staff hold.

- Working with the facilitator, select about six people (three in small organisations) who have imagination and an understanding of the changing environment that the organisation operates in. At least one of the team needs to be a technology expert.

- Brief the team on the aims of the exercise. Specify the variables that you particularly wish to explore, e.g. inflation rates, leaving the European Union, rejoining the EU!

- Don't try to look too far into the future. As previously indicated, anything over three years is about as accurate as an astrological chart.

- Working alone, ask every member of the team to prepare a list of the issues that they see arising from the variables given. Allow people to add new variables to their list. Give them about a week to think about their list and to briefly write up their ideas.

- Circulate each person's report to every member of the team in advance. At the meeting, allow for between 30 and 60 minutes to discuss each submission. If you want everyone to say what they are thinking, including seemingly daft ideas, avoid criticism of ideas at this stage. Analyse the ideas discussed using risk and cost as descriptors Vis:

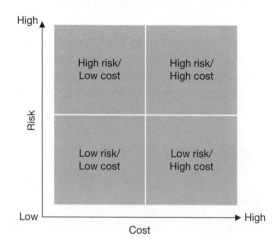

- Clearly, it's not worth working up strategies for low risk/low cost or high risk/low cost scenarios. Concentrate your efforts on low risk/high cost and high risk/high cost. If any issue in these two categories has a 30 per cent chance or more of occurring, you need to determine a strategy for how to deal with it.
- It's very likely that a single strategy will address several scenarios. It is these strategies that you should work up in greatest detail as they are the most likely to be used in practice.
- For each scenario, develop a best and worst case scenario and one midpoint between those.
- Report your finding to senior management/board and get their approval for your recommendations. This will save time if you have to implement one or more strategies in the future.

QUESTIONS TO ASK

- Given a free hand, who in the organisation would I like on the scenario team?
- Is there anyone in the organisation I can appoint as facilitator or do I need to go outside for the right person?

QUOTATION 68 # MICHAEL E. PORTER ON SETTING YOUR STRATEGY

Use this to help you set clear unambiguous targets.

Michael E. Porter (b. 1947) during his time at Harvard Business School has built a reputation as economist, researcher, author and lecturer. He is, perhaps, most famous for his Five Forces Theory Model, which is a framework for organisational analysis and strategic development. He has said that:

> Sound strategy starts with having the right goal.
>
> [and]
>
> The essence of strategy is choosing what not to do.
>
> **Michael E. Porter**

The above quotation contains two separate, but linked, messages.

WHAT TO DO

- A great number of managers think that it's so obvious what the organisation's overall goal is that it's not worth considering it in any detail. That's a mistake. Organisations change, sometimes quickly sometimes at the speed of a glacier. But they change. Therefore, every organisation should annually/bi-annually reconsider and agree what their major goal is.

- Obviously there will be a series of lower level goals and targets to be met if the organisation's major goal/s is/are to be achieved. Unfortunately, some managers fail to breakdown the organisation's goal/s into targets that are meaningful for staff. This lack of clarity means that staff don't fully appreciate how their work fits into the organisation's overall goals (see Quotation 44). This can lead to confusion and sub-optimisation. Each organisational goal needs to be defined and communicated clearly to all staff responsible for its achievement, and managers must then break it down into a series of targets for their staff.

- Use the SMART target-setting approach when defining your targets and those of your staff, i.e. all goals must be:
  - Specific
  - Measurable
  - Achievable
  - Realistic
  - Timely, (with a specified deadline).
- Often the biggest problem with goal or target setting is that managers want to measure and control every little thing. Learn to say no. Follow Jack Walsh's advice (see Quotation 30) and concentrate on a few key goals and targets. Fewer goals means that greater attention will be given to each one, which increases the likelihood that it will be achieved.
- The ability to say no will ensure that only projects central to the organisation's goals will be sanctioned. However, you need to balance such tight control with the need to take account of changing conditions and unexpected events (see Quotation 65) for new ideas and directions to be identified and evaluated.

QUESTIONS TO ASK

- Do I and my staff know what the organisation's goals are and understand the part that we play in their achievement?
- How precise/clear are the targets I set for myself and my staff?

QUOTATION 69 # WINSTON CHURCHILL ON THE NEED TO EVALUATE YOUR STRATEGY (TOP TEN ENTRY)

Use this to remind you of the value of post-implementation reviews.

Winston Churchill (1874–1965) was recently voted the greatest Briton of all time. He was a statesman, author, orator and Nobel laureate. He also minted numerous phrases that will live as long as English is spoken. The quotation below is not one of his best. However, it does emphasise the need for all organisations to conduct a review of how successful their decisions and strategy have been and learn from both its success and failures.

> However beautiful the strategy, you should occasionally look at the results.
>
> **Winston Churchill**

WHAT TO DO

- Many years ago, when I was studying to be an accountant, one of the hot issues of the day was the failure of British industry to carry out post-implementation reviews of its decisions. Forty years on, nothing much has changed. It is still the case that many companies undertake little or no post-implementation reviews of decisions taken or strategies implemented. People argue that they don't have the time to undertake such reviews. But I'm inclined to think it's a case of self-preservation. They don't want to be held accountable for poor decisions. This is a shame because by failing to review both their successes and failures they are foregoing a truly wonderful learning opportunity. Always undertake a review. Even if the findings are *'For your eyes only, Mr . . . '*
- When reviewing a successful decision or strategy, consider the following:
  - To what extent was the success due to unanticipated outside factors?
  - Would the decision have been a failure without these external factors?

- Why didn't I identify these external factors in my decision-/strategy-making process?
- Did I maximise the benefits of these unexpected factors or was I slow to react to them?
- How can I improve my data collection to minimise the chances that I miss similar information in the future?
- What approaches, ideas and lessons (best practice) can I take from this successful decision/strategy and apply in the future and share with colleagues?

■ In the case of unsuccessful decisions and strategies:
- To what extent did unforeseen events blow me off course?
- Should I have been able to anticipate these unforeseen events? If so, why didn't I pick up on them? Was it to do with the process of data collection that I used or my own ego?
- Did I spend enough time examining the risks associated with the decision or strategy and developing strategies to deal with them should they occur (see Quotation 67)?
- What lesson can I learn from the failure and pass on to colleagues?

■ These evaluations don't have to be formal or lengthy. However, you should make a note of the key findings in your learning journal. This will help you to improve future performance and add valuable data to your store of tacit knowledge.

QUESTIONS TO ASK

■ Does the organisation have a policy of undertaking post-implementation reviews? If not, why not?

■ Like surgeons, do I bury my mistakes or learn from them? (To be fair to surgeons, they've always done both.)

CONCLUSION

It's said that we learn from our mistakes. I'm not so sure that we do. Or at least I'm not so sure that everyone does. The people that learn from their mistakes are those who take the trouble to reflect on what went wrong and what they need to do differently if they are to avoid making the same mistake in the future. That's valuable learning, which is why I choose Churchill's quotation for inclusion in the Top Ten:

> However beautiful the strategy, you should occasionally look at the results.
>
> **Winston Churchill**

While it's good to learn from our mistakes, we should also learn from our successes. Golf is a mysterious game and no one will ever know all its secrets. Perhaps that's why many good players immediately go through the motions of any good shot that they have just made. They are trying to programme their muscles with the memory of their great chip to the ninth or putt on the eighteenth in the hope that it will be there for them to access the next time they need it. You should do the same. Analyse why certain decisions and actions that you took were successful and call on that knowledge when faced with a similar situation in the future.

ONE LESSON TO TAKE AWAY

All planning is inherently inaccurate. Therefore, don't spend a ridiculous amount of time and resources trying to achieve 99 per cent accuracy. You're chasing a chimera. Settle for a reasonable level of accuracy and have contingency plans in place to deal with possible foreseen problems and a well-trained, flexible and fleet-footed staff to deal with totally unanticipated events.

SECTION 9

POWER AND INFLUENCE

INTRODUCTION

It used to be that it was impolite to talk about sex, politics or religion in social settings. Today, power seems to have replaced sex as the no-go area in polite society. In the age of equality, no one wants to talk about it, let alone admit that they exercise power over other people. Yet political and managerial power continues to exist. Every employer has the power to dismiss a member of staff, and statistics show that most people who lose their job are only about four pay packets away from severe financial difficulty. This means that managers have the potential to exercise very significant power over their staff if they decide to use it.

In this section, Quotation/s:

- 70 to 72 discuss the three types of control that they can exercise over people, namely authority, power and influence.

- 73 gives some guidance on how to survive an attack from someone with more power than you.

- 74 argues that there are times in every person's life when managers will be called upon to stand up to those in authority and/or those who wish to maintain the status quo if they are to achieve something that is of profound importance to them.

- 75 shows how easy it is to lose power.

Finally, as you read this section, you might want to reflect on how you are going to exercise the power that you have. Are you going to make it obvious to everyone that you possess power or are you going to keep in mind what Prince Charles said about power:

> The less people know about what is really going on, the easier it is to wield power and authority.
>
> **Prince Charles**

Provided you achieve your objectives, do you really want to tell people that I'm the "decider", as President George W. Bush said, and catch all the grief that goes with that particular title?

It's also worth remembering that the more you talk about your power, the less credibility you'll have. For, as Margaret Thatcher said:

> Power is like being a lady . . . if you have to tell people you are, you aren't.
>
> **Margaret Thatcher**

QUOTATION 70 MAX WEBER ON AUTHORITY

Use this to identify the different forms of authority that are available to you as a manager.

Karl Emil Maximilian (Max) Weber (1864–1920) was a German sociologist philosopher and political economist whose work has had a major influence on social theory and social research. He identified three forms of authority

> [Charismatic authority is an] extraordinary and personal gift of grace; [he distinguished charisma from the other forms of authority by stating that] Men do not obey him [the charismatic ruler] by virtue of tradition or statute, but because they believe in him.
>
> [Tradition is] the authority of the eternal yesterday.
>
> [Legal authority is the product of] rationally created rules.
>
> **Max Weber**

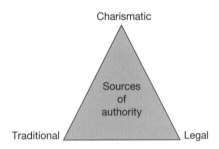

WHAT TO DO

- Under each heading, identify the level of power that you have.
  - Don't assume you lack charismatic power. You don't have to be an extrovert showman to possess charisma. People are drawn to leaders they admire, who display integrity and demonstrate that they care for their followers (see Quotation 36).
  - Traditional authority is based on family ties or 'membership of a special group'. Where an organisation is run by a family or members of a special group, you are very unlikely to rise to the top of the organisation unless you join the club by marrying into the family or gaining admittance to the club.

- Your legal rational authority is dependent on the position you hold, e.g. as team leader/manager/member of the board.
- Recognise that most managers possess very little traditional power. All managers have at least some charisma, i.e. the quality that marked you out as management material. All managers have a degree of legal rational power depending on their seniority.

- Work on increasing your charismatic power (see Quotation 71).

- Decide whether you really want to work in a place where traditional authority rules and an accident of birth or which 'club' you belong to defines your fate.

- Identify the limits of your legal rational power and be willing to use it to the limit. It is very rare for a manager to be told that they have exceeded their power. Staff like to be led by a 'powerful leader'. Senior managers are crying out for managers that will take things by the scruff of the neck and achieve results. But beware if things go wrong: that's when you'll be held to account for exceeding your power.

- Either use your power or lose it. Some managers are uncomfortable telling people what to do. That is pure nonsense. Your whole purpose as a manager is to direct people's actions. If you don't, your staff will ignore you.

QUESTIONS TO ASK

- Am I worried about telling people what to do? If so, where does this concern come from and what am I going to do about it?

- What charismatic power do I possess (honesty, integrity, loyalty, sociability, humour, care for staff) and how can I increase it?

QUOTATION 71 JOHN FRENCH JR AND BERTRAM RAVEN ON THE FIVE SOURCES OF SOCIAL POWER

Use this to identify the sources and level of power you have access to.

French and Raven wrote a seminal article in 1960 on the sources of social power. The following quotation refers to their most significant finding, i.e. that when you can access different sources of power, synergy occurs and your power expands significantly:

> We shall point out the interrelationships between different types of power, and the effects . . . one type of power [has] upon [the] other bases of power [you possess].
>
> **John French Jr and Bertram Raven**

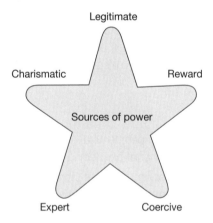

The five sources of power identified by French and Raven are:

- **Charismatic** power, i.e. the power of personality. It is the leader's personality that attracts the follower who wishes to identify with the leader and imitate their behaviour.
- **Legitimate** or positional power. Such power derives from the post held by the person in the organisation and is relinquished when they give up that position.
- **Expert** power comes from the person's possession of expert knowledge or skills that others do not possess. When these skills are no longer required, the person loses power.

- **Coercive** power is the ability to threaten others with a sanction and to impose that sanction if they fail to comply with the leader's wishes, e.g. sack someone.
- **Reward** power is the opposite to coercive power as it is the ability to reward a person, e.g. give them a raise or promotion.

WHAT TO DO

- Accumulate as many sources of power as you can because, when you access two or more sources, synergy occurs, a case of $2 + 2 = 5$. Stalin achieved and maintained his power through position, expert knowledge of the party, bureaucracy and coercive power.
- Alas, few of us have the charisma of a Tom Hiddleston or Adele. However, charisma lies in the eye of the beholder. Therefore, think about how you present yourself to staff, colleagues and others (see Quotation 13). If you act with confidence, honesty, fairness, integrity and humour, people will respect you and that is the first step on the way to charisma. Supply a compelling vision or philosophy and you are there.
- Identify the limits of your legitimate or positional power. Act as if you expect people to obey your instruction and avoid appearing diffident. No one will tell you what your limits of power are until you exceed them. So keep pushing until someone says stop.
- Identify what expert power you have. If you have a professional qualification in, say, accounting, law or engineering, think about adding to it with a further qualification that will enable you to fill a skill/ knowledge gap in the organisation.
- Identify the limits of your coercive power. Don't use coercive power to bully or intimidate people. Instead, demonstrate that you are willing to discipline or sack people when necessary. Do this once and afterwards you'll find that a quiet chat will sort most people out.
- Identify the rewards you can offer staff. These need not be financial. Staff often value the belief that you listen to their advice or have influence with you.

QUESTIONS TO ASK

- What sources of power do I currently have? Do I use them all?
- What other sources of power could I accumulate?

QUOTATION 72 ROBIN SHARMA ON THE POWER OF INFLUENCE

Use this as your default approach to gaining control over staff.

Robin S. Sharma (b. 1965) is an author and the founder of Sharma Leadership Consultancy. The following quotation of his identifies the difference between hard power and soft influence:

> Leadership is . . . about impact, influence and inspiration. Impact involves getting results, influence is about spreading the passion you have for your work, and you have to inspire team-mates and customers.
>
> **Robin Sharma**

Power can be used to compel people to do as you request. However, it can create a culture of fear and produce unhappy working conditions. On the other hand, influence seeks to persuade people to do as you request. It may take longer to achieve results but it creates a more harmonious relationship between manager and staff.

WHAT TO DO

- Only resort to power if influence fails. In times of genuine emergency go straight to power.
- Prepare the ground for using influence effectively by creating a good relation with each member of staff. Show an interest in their work, career, training, family, pastimes. But, most importantly, find out what motivates them and supply it.
- Identify the common interests and/or shared history you have with your staff, e.g. did you go to the same school, university? Do you have the same interests such as music or football? Did you share a similar training experience?
- Let people believe that you are one of them. People respond better to people whom they think share their values and beliefs. If you appear too intelligent, they will wonder whether you can ever really understand them.
- Make people feel relaxed and comfortable in your presence. Show that you are interested in what they have to say by using active

listening, e.g. asking questions and seeking clarification about what they've said. This is a much better way to influence people than talking at them.

■ Allow staff to play a part in any decision that affects them (see Quotations 51 and 54), however small. This reassures the person and they feel respected and valued. They are then more likely to support your decision.

■ Use reciprocity and exchange favours, e.g. 'If you work over an hour tonight, you can leave early on Friday.'

■ Demonstrate your expert knowledge, without showing off, and people will be impressed and more willing to listen to you when discussing anything that is covered by your expertise.

■ Seek out the views and opinions of staff and praise them for their ideas and insights when appropriate.

■ Try to arrive at a win/win solution rather than seeking a win/lose result when dealing with staff. There is nothing unethical in using a bit of reward power to win their co-operation (see Quotation 71). Just ensure that you don't let staff charge too high a price for their co-operation.

QUESTIONS TO ASK

■ Who are the unofficial staff leaders that I need to influence?

■ If I get the unofficial leaders on board, will they deliver the staff's support or do I also need to work directly on the staff myself?

QUOTATION 73 # NICCOLÒ MACHIAVELLI ON SURVIVAL

Use this to help you survive shifting political fortunes in your organisation.

Niccolò Machiavelli (1469–1527) was a statesman, diplomat and author during dangerous times and is lauded by many as the founder of modern political science. The advice he provides in his most famous book, *The Prince,* was intended to help a leader survive:

> The lion cannot protect himself from traps, and the fox cannot defend himself from wolves. One must therefore be a fox to recognise traps, and a lion to frighten wolves.
>
> **Niccolò Machiavelli**

You have to decide whether you want to use Machiavelli's advice for offensive purposes. However, in what follows, I have outlined how you need to be a fox most of the time and a lion occasionally if you are to survive.

WHAT TO DO

- Never delude yourself or allow others to mislead you with flattery. You must recognise the reality that you are faced with and act accordingly. Only then can you deal effectively with present threats/traps and plan for the future.

- Never cease thinking and working. If you have time on your hands, use it to identify both personal and organisational strengths, weaknesses, opportunities and threats and plan for how to deal with them when they arise.

- Never trust a friend; it's safer to place your trust in an old enemy. Friends often become resentful when you fail to properly recognise the role they played in helping you achieve the power/position you have. Whereas, if you have made peace with an old enemy, and now treat them as a friend, they will be grateful and constantly seek to demonstrate their loyalty to you.

- If you helped someone into power, beware. Many leaders will seek to eliminate those that helped them. Why? Because they pose a risk if they become resentful of the leader's new pre-eminence and come to believe that they should be the leader.

- If you work for someone who believes that the ends justify the means, they will not think twice about dumping you if you cease to be useful to them. Therefore find what they need and supply it, and never give them any reason to doubt your loyalty.

- If you join a new organisation, assert your power and eliminate any threats to you by destroying any remnants of the old regime. If you are a member of the old regime, demonstrate your loyalty to the new leader by making yourself indispensable to them.

- Eliminate all threats to your position before they have a chance to grow to dangerous proportions. Many new senior managers change their entire management team within a year of appointment as a way of stamping their authority on the organisation and staff.

QUESTIONS TO ASK

- How Machiavellian am I in how I deal with people and situations?
- Do I know enough about the power games that people play and how to protect myself?

QUOTATION 74

ALBERT EINSTEIN ON WHY YOU SHOULD FIGHT AUTHORITY

Use this to remind you of the need to overturn the status quo when necessary.

Albert Einstein (1879–1955) was probably the best known scientist of the twentieth century. As a scientist he recognised that progress could be achieved only by challenging current orthodoxies which were upheld by those institutions and individuals that had a vested interest in maintaining the status quo. It is for this reason that he said:

> Unthinking respect for authority is the greatest enemy of truth.
>
> **Albert Einstein**

It is in challenging the status quo and trying out new ideas that great managers are created. I've used an example of a change in what follows as most disputes are about changing the status quo.

WHAT TO DO

- If you ever ask someone, 'Why do you do it like that?', and they reply, 'Because we've always done it like that', then it's £50 to a rusty washer that you've discovered a process ripe for change. You might also want to look at the person who made the comment!
- Don't change things just for the sake of it or to improve the look of your CV (see Quotation 61). Only change when it's required.
- Don't be put off if the powers that be or your own staff challenge you. They often have a vested interest in stopping change and, the louder they squeal, the more likely it is that they see your change as a threat to their current comfortable position.
- Identify the forces that are likely to support or oppose your change and assess the relative power of those who will support and oppose you (see Quotation 61).

■ Remember that where someone can draw on several sources of power, synergy occurs and they are likely to be formidable enemies or allies (see Quotation 71).

■ Use Lewin's Force Field analysis to identify the forces in favour of change and those opposed to it.

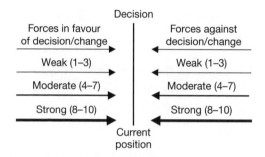

■ Start by taking a piece of paper and drawing a line down the centre. On the left of the line, list the forces that oppose you and score each force. On the right, list the forces for change and score them.

■ Once you have the schedule, consider how you can weaken/undermine the forces against change. On the right, identify how supporting forces can be strengthened and added to. This is where knowing where power resides in the organisation is invaluable. If you can convince/influence key individuals to join your side, then they may well bring other supporters with them.

■ Don't announce your idea or suggestion until you are convinced that: (i) you have identified all its potential weaknesses and have an answer for how you will address them, and (ii) you hold a balance of power over your opponents. If necessary, delay while you gather more support.

QUESTIONS TO ASK

■ Do I know who has power in my organisation?

■ Have I done enough lobbying and networking with managers and colleagues to gain their support?

QUOTATION 75

ROSABETH MOSS KANTER AND SOPHOCLES ON HOW TO LOSE POWER (TOP TEN ENTRY)

Use this to remind you how easy it is to lose power because of your own actions.

Rosabeth Moss Kanter (b. 1943), Professor of Business at Harvard Business School, is perhaps best known for her work on change management. Change invariably means altering what is currently in existence, and to do that you need power. For, as she has said:

> Power is the ability to get things done.
>
> **Rosabeth Moss Kanter**

The great Greek playwright Sophocles provides a counterpoint to the above quotation with his statement that a leader should:

> Never command what you cannot enforce.
>
> **Sophocles**

The connection between these two quotations is explored below.

WHAT TO DO

- If you exercise your power and then find that you can't enforce your wishes, you will lose power. An inability to command compliance destroys a person's power almost as quickly as a successful coup. It must be avoided at all costs, so only fight the fights you can win.
- If power is the ability to get things done, then refusing to do anything with your power is, perhaps, the second quickest way to lose it. As a manager, you have certain sources of power (see Quotations 70–72), but, if you never exercise it, it becomes dulled and blunt. You need to use it to keep it sharp.

- From the moment you are appointed to a particular position, you need to demonstrate your power. People will be looking to see what you do. They will quickly make judgements about you and, even if wrong, they will hamper you while you address the misconceptions. One way to avoid this is to do something to announce your arrival. What that might be will depend on the sources of power you can call upon (see Quotation 71) and your position in the organisation. But don't announce, emphasise or dwell on whatever you do. The more effortless your action seems, the more impact it will have on people.

- Many people in Great Britain, and other countries, find it difficult and embarrassing to tell people what to do. It's not part of their upbringing or social culture. Get over it! Management is hard enough without tying one hand behind your back. Power is one of the most effective weapons that you have in your arsenal. It should not be your weapon of first choice, but when all else fails you must be willing to use it to compel compliance with your directions. You'll find this incredibly difficult to do unless you regularly exercise the powers you have.

- Don't resort to coercive power as your first choice if an instruction is ignored. To use coercive compliance too early actually undermines your credibility with staff and colleagues. Think of coercion as your nuclear option and only use as a last resort – but always be willing to use it if all else fails.

- If it's just one person that opposes you, deal with them behind closed doors. If a group led by one person opposes you, deal with him/her in front of the group. Nasty, maybe. Effective, definitely.

QUESTIONS TO ASK

- Do I have a problem giving orders and enforcing compliance?
- Is there any particular person or group that opposes my instruction? How can I neutralise them?

CONCLUSION

I've selected Quotation 75, with its two quotations, as my Top Ten entry because combined they offer a warning to managers about how easy it is to lose power.

> Power is the ability to get things done.
>
> **Rosabeth Moss Kanter**

However, any reticence or failure on a manager's part to use their power will lead to it withering away to such an extent that when they try exercise it people will just ignore them.

Sophocles reminds managers that they should:

> Never command what you cannot enforce.
>
> **Sophocles**

An inability to implement your instructions or commands kills a manager's credibility stone-dead with both staff and colleagues. So, never issue any order or instruction if there is any doubt at all about your ability to enforce it.

Margaret Thatcher, perhaps the most obviously powerful prime minister of the last 70 years, forgot this principle and never recovered from her inability to implement the poll tax.

ONE LESSON TO TAKE AWAY

As a manager you must identify your sources of authority, power and influence and the level at which you can exercise them. Once this is done you need to protect, preserve and extend you power bases. Failing to use your power when required will lead to loss of power.

SECTION 10

TURNING CUSTOMERS INTO PARTNERS

INTRODUCTION

M ichael Dell was supporting and emphasising Peter Drucker's belief that the main purpose of any company is to create a customer (see Quotation 1) when he said:

Customers are your future, representing new opportunities, ideas and avenues for growth.

Michael Dell

If you lose sight of this fundamental law of commerce, then you and your organisation will suffer. The seven entries in this section are all about building, maintaining and protecting your relationship with your customers. Quotation/s:

- 76 is a reality check, in case you need one, which emphasises your dependency on customers for survival.
- 77 suggests that in any relationship the spotlight should be on them and not you.
- 78 outlines how valuable unhappy customers are to you in any attempt to improve your service and goods.
- 79 to 81 are each, in their own way, concerned with building and maintaining a good relationship with your customers.
- 82 considers how benchmarking can be used to provide a better service to your customers.

As you read the entries, put yourself in the shoes of your customers. Would you be happy with the goods, service and treatment you receive from your organisation, or would you feel as if the organisation sees you as a cash cow and nothing more than an inconvenient nuisance when you complain?

CLAYTON M. CHRISTENSEN ON HOW CUSTOMERS CONTROL YOUR ORGANISATION

Use this to remind you and your staff that happy customers are your greatest asset.

Clayton M. Christensen (b. 1952) is an American academic, educator, author and business consultant. His management interests are wide-ranging but he captured just how important customers are to an organisation when he said:

> It is a company's customers who effectively control what it can and can't do.
>
> **Clayton M. Christensen**

At the start of this section on how to build and maintain customer relations, it's worth emphasising that you are not doing your customers a favour by providing them with a great service. It is actually they who hold the power in this relationship.

WHAT TO DO

- In large organisations there is a danger that too many people become remote from customers. It would be useful if every organisation followed the advice of Robert Townsend and required all staff to spend two weeks working on the front line dealing with customers when first appointed and every three or four years thereafter.

- Commit your organisation to placing customers at the centre of all you do. Make their satisfaction your focus. Now some of you may say: I don't have anything to do with customers, I work in IT or R&D. Well, you do have customers. The people within the organisation who receive your reports or services are your customers and you should treat them as such. If you provide a poor service, word will quickly spread and you'll find yourself under pressure to improve or leave.

- Train all staff, including senior staff, in the organisation's customer care policy and procedures. If senior staff attend the same training sessions as middle and junior staff, it will send out a more powerful message about the importance of customer care than any number of emails and pronouncements they make from on high.

■ Aim to ensure that anyone in the organisation who receives a complaint is able to deal with it and not just 'transfer the call' to customer services and wash their hands of it.

■ As part of the training, explain how the customers' actions effectively control what the organisation is able to do. Too often staff forget the simple truth that it is customers who pay their wages and provide the profits for investment in new machinery, systems and research.

■ Don't allow staff to talk disparagingly of customers. Yes, there is always the funny story that can and should be shared, but denigration of customers by staff should not be tolerated. It's a sign of contempt and, if widespread, becomes part of the organisation's culture and accepted practice. Such entrenched attitudes are then difficult to eradicate.

■ Choose from the quotations in this section those ideas that you find useful and incorporate them into your own customer procedures.

QUESTIONS TO ASK

■ How much attention do I give to issues of customer care?

■ Do I think that customer care is boring and switch off as soon as anyone mentions customer care, thinking that it doesn't affect me?

QUOTATION 77 # DALE CARNEGIE ON WHY IT'S NOT ABOUT YOU (TOP TEN ENTRY)

Use this to remind you of the importance of establishing good lines of communication with your customers.

Dale Carnegie (1888–1955) wrote the bestselling management book of all time, *How to Win Friends and Influence People.* The book has been described as the salesperson's bible. But the book is about much more than just sales. It's concerned with how to build and maintain relationships which is the foundation of all good business practices.

> You can close more business in two months by becoming interested in other people than you can in two years by trying to get people interested in you.
>
> **Dale Carnegie**

We all love to talk about ourselves, our triumphs and problems. Is it any wonder that we like people who are willing to listen?

WHAT TO DO

- You have two ears and one mouth. Therefore, spend twice as much time listening to your customers than talking at them. This will improve your relationship with them and your sales will increase.

- Let your customer set the agenda. Encourage them to talk about their business, your products and products from other suppliers. If you're really lucky, they will tell you what they wish you made. This will help you to identify their true needs and may lead to the alteration of existing products or the development of new ones.

- Remember, you'll never learn anything new when you do the talking. All new knowledge is obtained by listening. So learn to listen actively. Don't sit there thinking about what you are going to say when the other person stops talking. Listen, then ask questions about what they said and/or seek further information or clarification. This will show that you are interested in what they have to say.

- Stay in contact with your customers. Communicate with them regularly, even when you're not trying to sell them something. Who knows, they may mention a problem that you might be able to help them with and, bingo, an unexpected sale is made to a grateful customer. Use email, phone, newsletters, personal visits and social events to develop your relationship.

- Build trust. Always keep your word. Don't renege on a deal or a promise, even if it means you lose money. Give your best customers your best deals, don't exploit them.
- Be frank with customers. If there is a problem, tell them as soon as you know about it. If you can't answer a question don't bluff. Tell them you don't know but you'll find out and get back to them.
- Don't become defensive when customers become critical. See it as an opportunity to rebuild good relations by sorting out any problem to their satisfaction.
- Recognise customer loyalty by offering a range of rewards, including discounts, better payment terms and special deals.
- Build up a profile for each customer and spot developing trends.

QUESTIONS TO ASK

- How often do I speak to/visit my customers?
- Do I always ensure that my customers get the best deals going or do I give those to new customers?

QUOTATION 78 # BILL GATES ON WHAT YOU CAN LEARN FROM UNHAPPY CUSTOMERS

Use this to remind you that dissatisfied customers are your best source of information.

Bill Gates (b. 1955), Co-founder of Microsoft, businessman and philan-thropist, believes that:

> Your most unhappy customers are your greatest source of learning.
>
> **Bill Gates**

Nobody likes to be criticised but, if you can park your ego and just listen to what people are telling you, without becoming defensive, you can learn a lot.

WHAT TO DO

■ As suggested in Quotation 77, you have two ears and one mouth and you should use them in that proportion, especially when dealing with an unhappy customer.

■ Train everyone in how to deal with customer complaints, even if the organisation has a specialist complaints team. You can never predict when or where a customer will raise a complaint.

■ Make it simple for the customer to speak to or see a living, breathing person and not have to put up with a pre-recorded message or a long wait.

■ If you use a call centre, demand that all staff are properly trained and that you/your staff have oversight of that training. Don't accept the situation where staff simply read from a script.

■ If possible, locate the centre within the borders of Great Britain or whichever country you operate from. People don't want to talk to someone on the other side of the world and they certainly don't want to divulge sensitive information. Benchmark your service against the service provided by First Direct Bank (see Quotation 82).

- Always acknowledge the customer's anger and apologise. Don't become defensive. The criticism isn't personal.
- More than anything, irate customers want to (a) express their annoyance/anger and (b) have their problem resolved. You can't resolve the issue until you identify exactly what the issue is. So, listen carefully and, when they have finished, feed back to the customer what you think the problem is, e.g. 'So what you're saying is xyz.'
- Ask questions and clarify any issues that are unclear. Unless the conversation is being recorded, keep a note of what is said.
- Ask the customer what they want done to resolve the problem. Many people just want an apology and a replacement product and recompense for any costs they have incurred. This is a small price to pay for placating a customer and maintaining their loyalty.
- If you can't resolve the problem immediately, tell the customer what you are going to do, when you are going to get back to them and then deliver on your promise.
- If you have done all of the above, then you will have a detailed and accurate record of the complaint. Record that information and analyse it weekly or monthly. Look for:
  - patterns that might indicate a reoccurring problem – if one is spotted, you need to deal with it at source;
  - ideas for how to improve your product/service;
  - ideas for new products;
  - information about what your competitors are doing and products they are developing.

QUESTIONS TO ASK

- How often do I review customer complaints?
- Do I take criticism personally and/or defensively?

QUOTATION 79 | # TOM PETERS ON WHY YOU SHOULD ALWAYS UNDER-PROMISE AND OVER-DELIVER

Use this to improve customer perceptions of you and your organisation.

Tom Peters (b. 1942), possibly the most successful management guru of the late twentieth century, is interested in a wide array of management topics but none more so than customer care. To keep customers satisfied, he suggested that businesses should always:

> Under-promise and over-deliver
>
> **Tom Peters**

WHAT TO DO

- Don't make grandiose claims for your products. That's just setting the customer up for a disappointment and, possibly, a complaint. Either way, it's probable that they will never trust your organisation again.
- Identify the ways in which you can over deliver. For example:
  - Deliver the goods sooner than expected.
  - Pass on a percentage of any savings that arise between the order being placed and the goods delivered (yes, I know that's unusual but think of the impact on your customers).
  - Produce goods of unexpected quality for the price: Tissot, Skoda and Victorinox are all manufacturers that manage to provide a first-class product at reasonable prices.
  - Provide a great after-care service. The customer's experience of your product extends over its entire life, therefore great customer care after delivery is not a luxury add-on but an essential part of your service.
  - Deal with complaints and returns promptly (see Quotation 77). Never argue with the customer; do what's required to settle their problem. Then when they tell the story of their broken widget, the outcome is a happy one that reflects well on your organisation;

instead of the incident undermining the customer's loyalty to your organisation, they become one of its greatest advocates.

- As a matter of policy, always uphold the spirit of any agreement that you enter into with staff, customers and suppliers, not just the word of the agreement. This will delight your customers, scare the hell out of your competitors and win you friends and new customers.

■ Surprise established customers with special offers and increased discounts. Don't advertise them in advance: just drop it on them out of the blue. That will get them talking about you.

■ Be loyal to your customers. If they are in temporary difficulties, try and help them out. They will remember it. It will cement your relationship with them and if, one day, you experience difficulties, they may be able to help you.

QUESTIONS TO ASK

■ As a strategy, in my own career, do I always try to under-promise and then over-deliver?

■ How often do I or my organisation over-deliver to our customers?

QUOTATION 80

WARREN BUFFET ON HOW TO LOSE YOUR REPUTATION

Use this to remind you that one misstep can ruin your business and reputation overnight.

Warren Buffet (b. 1930) isn't just the canniest investor in history, he is also a businessman who built up Hathaway Investments from a $100 organisation in the 1950s to a multibillion-dollar investment organisation. A man of great integrity, his organisation enjoys a truly phenomenal reputation amongst both its shareholders and the organisations he invests in. It's therefore not surprising that he has something to say about personal and organisational reputations:

> It takes 20 years to build a reputation and 5 minutes to ruin it. If you think about that, you'll do things differently.
>
> **Warren Buffet**

In business, a reputation for keeping absolutely to the letter and spirit of an agreement, even when it disadvantages you, is the most precious asset any organisation can hold.

WHAT TO DO

- Does your reputation provide you with a competitive advantage (see Quotation 2)? Remember, for a competitive advantage to exist, your reputation has to be better than that of your competitors. Being equal to is not an advantage.

- Identify the reputation you want to build for yourself and your organisation. Assuming that you are not a drug dealer or gangland overlord, you'll want to be known for your honesty, fairness to staff, customers, suppliers and shareholders; never cheating, misleading or exploiting staff, customers or suppliers; being a person or organisation that not only honours the word of your contracts but the spirit also. Claiming that you do these things isn't enough; you'll have to demonstrate your commitment to them over an extended period of time. But once your reputation has been established, it will lead to better and more lucrative business deals.

- If you want to lose your reputation overnight, you will only have to be found, lying, cheating, being dishonest or disparaging about your customers, suppliers or shareholders once and you'll find yourself spending thousands, perhaps millions, on public relations. Think of BP and the Deep Water Horizon disaster and its appalling initial reaction to the spillage. Or Gerald Ratner who confided at a business meeting that the reason he could sell a decanter, glasses and tray for £4.99 was because it was crap. Unfortunately, even in a time before social media, his gaffe was so bad it made every news broadcast in the UK, and the Ratner's brand disappeared from the high street within a year. His gaffe has become a textbook example of the dangers of treating your customers with contempt, even when it's meant only in jest.
- Should you have a slip, then apologise immediately, come clean and compensate (see Quotation 78).
- If you have a mentor in the organisation or have a colleague you trust, discuss with them your reputation within the organisation.

QUESTIONS TO ASK

- Am I happy with my reputation or do I need to improve it?
- Am I happy with the reputation my team have or do I need to improve it?

JEFF BEZOS ON THE IMPLICATIONS OF BAD NEWS IN THE DIGITAL AGE

Use this to remind you that your business is only one foul-up away from being an internet sensation.

Jeff Bezos (b. 1964), founder and CEO of Amazon.com, built a global empire based on new technology and dealing with customers via the internet. Therefore, we should listen when he tells us that:

> If someone thinks they are being mistreated by us, they won't tell 5 people, they'll tell 5,000.
>
> **Jeff Bezos**

WHAT TO DO

- Stop an error becoming a disaster. Settle the dispute before it becomes a war of attrition.
- If you identify a significant problem affecting numerous customers, go public with it on social networking sites immediately. It's better to reveal the problem than have hundreds of customers complain about you on Twitter or Facebook. But you must act quickly. *The Times* (4 November 2013) quoted a report that said 69 per cent of 'business crisis' spread internationally within 24 hours, while organisations took 21 hours, on average, to release their initial response.
- If you are a large organisation, employ experts to monitor what is being said about your organisation online. If you are a small organisation, the monitoring processes might involve one person spending an hour or so a day checking out what has been said about the organisation. Regardless of size, the important thing is to do the monitoring and respond to problems quickly.
- Don't allow social media to bully you. If the criticism is unfair or inaccurate, rebut the story. But always apologise for genuine errors and compensate quickly.
- Don't give the fire additional oxygen by entering into an argument with the complainant through the media. We all know that the press will be

on the side of the gallant small man/woman taking on big business – even if your firm employs only 25 people. Your aim should always be to contain and extinguish the fire as soon as possible.

- A memorable episode of *The West Wing* showed, in very amusing terms, what happens when the wrong person speaks to the press. You should have a list of people who are authorised to speak to the press and, equally important, a list of those who should be rugby-tackled, if necessary, to keep them away from a reporter or social network site. Every organisation has them and I'm sure you know who they are.

QUESTIONS TO ASK

- Does the organisation have a media policy? If so, do I and my staff know what it is?
- If I spot trouble brewing, do I know who I should speak to first?

QUOTATION 82 # WARREN BENNIS ON THE VALUE OF BENCHMARKING

Use this when you wish to compare your performance in a specific area of work with that of the market leader.

Warren Bennis (1925–2014) was an American academic, organisational consultant, author and a pioneer in the comparatively new field of Leadership Studies. He was also interested in the quality movement that blossomed in the 1990s and recommended that managers should copy best practice from other organisations, namely:

> Copying other organisations' activities sounds like industrial espionage . . . but the truth is benchmarking is perfectly legal and ethical.
>
> **Warren Bennis**

Benchmarking was developed by Fredrick Taylor in the early years of the twentieth century. Excellent factory workers were identified by placing a chalk mark on their bench or work station. The mark was public recognition that that person's work was of a high quality and should be copied by others. From such modest origins a multibillion-pound industry has grown.

There are four stages in any benchmarking process:

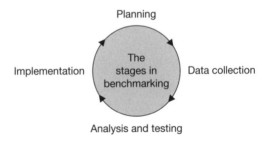

WHAT TO DO

■ Recognise that it is not necessary for you to compare yourself to organisations in the same industry. For example, anyone with a customer will benefit from studying Lexus Cars' approach to customer care.

- Use the following four-stage approach to undertake a benchmarking exercise.

    The planning stage identifies the processes that you wish to benchmark. Be as specific as you can, e.g. do you want to examine the entire process or just parts of it? Decide on which organisations have a reputation for excellence in that specific area and negotiate access to see 'how they do it'. Devise a suitable data-collection tool questionnaire, observation or interview schedule.

    Data-collection stage involves negotiating with the organisation you have identified, your level of access issues surrounding sensitive business data and any ethical considerations that might arise and how you will deal with them. No one involved in the study should be harmed in any way.

    The analysis and doing stage involves summarising and analysing the data and identifying any practices that might improve your organisation's performance. Do this with a small group of people, including one or two front-line staff who can act as change agents/champions (see Quotation 57). Test ideas on a small scale and amend as required. Start to involve as many staff as you can.

    The implementation stage is where you and your team implement the new ideas that you have identified. Leading up to the implementation and during the final roll-out, actively involve as many people as possible in the work. This gives them a sense of ownership and also enables you and your team to keep in close contact with all significant stakeholders. Use SMART targets (see Quotation 19) to monitor progress.

QUESTIONS TO ASK

- Am I genuinely interested in quality or is it just something I know I have to pay lip service to?
- Do I set a good example by always producing good quality work myself and expecting others to do the same?

CONCLUSION

I have chosen Quotation 77 by Dale Carnegie for inclusion in the Top Ten because it summarises the basis upon which you should build your relationship with customers, i.e.:

> You can close more business in two months by becoming interested in other people than you can in two years by trying to get people interested in you.
>
> **Dale Carnegie**

Don't hog the spotlight. Instead, put it on your customer and make them the star attraction in every meeting/conversation you have with them. Do this and they will think you are a wonderful conversationalist because you listened to them and they felt good about themselves as a result. Someone wanted to hear what they had to say! In a world where most people are seldom listened to, that's powerful stuff.

ONE LESSON TO TAKE AWAY

You will do more business and build better relationships with customers if you show a genuine interest in what they have to say about the problems, needs and ideas that they have.

SECTION 11

A MISCELLANY
OF WISDOM

INTRODUCTION

This section contains eight quotations which I think are important and insightful. Two characteristics that all of them share are: none of them fits neatly into any of the other sections; each is fairly self-explanatory and doesn't require a full two pages to explain what they mean or how to use them. Effectively, they are eight small, but perfectly formed, gems.

A typical example of the type of quotations used in this section comes from Robert Townsend who suggested that:

> Consultants are people who borrow your watch and tell you what time it is, and then walk off with your watch.
>
> **Robert Townsend**

You'll also note that there is no Top Ten entry from this section. The explanation for this omission is simple. Eleven into ten doesn't go!

Given the variety of quotations used in this section, it's difficult to suggest what to look for as you read the section. Perhaps the best thing to do is to identify the two or three quotations that speak directly to you and your experience of work.

QUOTATION 83 # ELVIS PRESLEY ON KNOWING WHICH EXPERTS YOU NEED

Use this to remind you to identify precisely the skills you need before appointing external consultants.

Elvis Aaron Presley (1935–77) was The King to his fans and a hugely significant cultural icon of the twentieth century. Elvis was not renowned for his business acumen; however, he showed more awareness of his real needs than many professional managers when he said:

> I have no use for bodyguards, but I have very specific use for two highly trained Certified Public Accountants.
>
> **Elvis Presley**

Elvis knew that the retinue he travelled with provided significant protection from fans and those wishing to harm him (he also carried a gun). So he didn't think he needed bodyguards. What he did require was protection from the Revenue Service.

WHAT TO DO

- Don't employ experts you don't need. Often, companies have the expertise in-house to research the problem they are struggling with. Unfortunately, many managers believe that an outside expert is bound to be better than anyone in-house. After all, they charge £1,000+ a day, they must be good. In many cases, this assumption is incorrect. Always check whether there is someone in the organisation who can do the job before going outside.
- Identify precisely the type of expertise that you require. Don't employ a generalist management consultant if what you really need is an IT or finance specialist. It's surprising how often this happens and is often caused by buying in non-accounting services from the accounting firm that does your audit.

QUESTIONS TO ASK

- Am I, or my organisation, enthralled by the concept of the all-wise management consultant?
- Do I use management consultants to promote my own agenda?

QUOTATION 84 # EILEEN C. SHAPIRO ON THE NEED TO AVOID MANAGEMENT FADS

Use this to remind you that ready-made solutions to your problems seldom work.

Eileen C. Shapiro is an American business consultant and author of *Fad Surfing in the Boardroom.* Shapiro is concerned with the growing trend in business to look outside the organisation for ready-made answers to its problems, as she has said:

> Thinking must be the hardest job in the World. What people want to do is outsource it to a mantra or methodology like re-engineering.
>
> **Eileen C. Shapiro**

In the 1980s, management became sexy as managers looked around for instant answers to age-old problems. The result has been a growing trend for managers to look outside their organisations for answers to their problems.

WHAT TO DO

- Thinking is hard, but you and your staff have the answers to the problems you face. You may need a facilitator to draw them out, but you are more than capable of designing a made-to-measure solution for resolving your problems.
- Off-the-peg solutions seldom deliver the results hoped for. However, if you or your organisation decide to go down that route, you need to do two things:
  - precisely identify the problem/s you are attempting to resolve; and
  - instead of swallowing the entire solution on offer, take only those elements that you require to solve your problem/s and that will work in your organisation's culture.
- Don't assume that you can implement any package without significant amendment. The package must be altered to meet your unique requirements.

QUESTIONS TO ASK

- Am I or is my organisation a slave to management fads?
- How much time do I spend just thinking through problems as opposed to dealing with them?

JOHN PIERPONT MORGAN ON WHY YOU SHOULD PROVIDE SOLUTIONS NOT PROBLEMS IN ANY REPORT

Use this to remind you that management want to know how to do things not reasons for why they can't.

John Pierpont (J.P.) Morgan (1837–1913) was an American financier and banker who dominated corporate finance and industrial consolidation in the United States during the latter part of the nineteenth century and into the twentieth. Morgan did not build his vast financial empire by taking no for an answer, as the following quotation demonstrates:

> I don't want a lawyer to tell me what I can't do. I hire people to tell me how to do what I want to do.
>
> **John Pierpont Morgan**

WHAT TO DO

- Always remember that organisations want managers who are problem solvers not problem creators.
- As an accountant, I've long recognised that there are two types of accountants: those that tell you why you can't do something and those that tell you how to do something. The same is true of most professions, including bankers and lawyers. When appointing staff or outside experts, pose them a business problem and ask them for their views on it. Say as little as possible beyond that. You would expect any good professional to list the difficulties that they see. However, the naysayers will spend a disproportionate amount of time outlining the problems compared to those who are more concerned with identifying a way forward. Appoint people from the latter group.

QUESTIONS TO ASK

- Do I place obstacles in the way of people wanting to do something or do I help them get around problems?
- Do my staff have a reputation for helping people resolve problems or for raising additional issues?

QUOTATION 86 # PETER DRUCKER ON THE VALUE OF THINKING AND REFLECTION

Use this as the ideal way to constantly improve your management skills.

Peter Drucker (1909–2005) was perhaps the most profound thinker that management science has produced. Therefore it's hardly surprising that he said:

> Follow effective action with quiet reflection. From the reflection will come even more effective action.
>
> **Peter Drucker**

WHAT TO DO

- Most managers are over-stretched and action-oriented. Reflection doesn't come easily to them. They'd rather be dealing with the latest problem and not thinking about the last. But failing to set time aside every day for quiet reflection is a mistake. Reflection will help you become a more effective manager which will save time in the long run.

- Keep a learning journal. Record in it significant incidents and decisions and very briefly analyse each one, e.g. What went well? What went badly? How can I improve on what I did next time? How can I build on the good stuff and eliminate the bad?

- If you don't have time to reflect on what you've done during work, spend ten or fifteen minutes on the commute home thinking about what happened during the day.

- By undertaking regular reflections, you will learn from both your successes and failures, with the result that when you retire people will say to you, 'The organisation is losing 45 years' valuable experience.' If you don't reflect on and learn from your experiences, they will say, 'There goes one year's experience repeated forty-five times!' Only not to your face.

QUESTIONS TO ASK

- In a week how much time do I spend reflecting on what I have done?
- Do I think reflection is for wimps? If so, why, when all the evidence shows it works?

QUOTATION 87 | # ABRAHAM MASLOW ON WHY YOU MUST BE THE BEST YOU CAN BE

Use this to remind you that you have only one life and shouldn't spend it doing a job you hate.

Abraham Maslow (1908–70) is most famous for creating his hierarchy of needs, the pinnacle of which is self-actualisation. Failing to at least try to achieve self-actualisation can result in disappointment and unhappiness namely:

> If you plan on being anything less than you are capable of being, you will probably be unhappy all the days of your life.
>
> **Abraham Maslow**

WHAT TO DO

- Identify which of the following groups you belong to: (A) the lucky few who knew from a very early age what they wanted to do, (B) the majority who learnt to become good at something that then becomes their life's work and (C) the rest who never find what they are good at/interested in.
- If you belong to either group A or B, then you are lucky. However, true happiness doesn't come from just doing what you want to, it is found in doing it to the absolute best of your abilities. So aim high. You may fail but that is more satisfying than aiming low and succeeding every time.
- The people in group C probably drifted into their job. Typically, they'll say, 'My job's OK. It pays the mortgage/rent.' If you are one of these, you need to ask yourself, 'Do I really want to spend the rest of my life doing this job?' If the answer is no, then identify what you want to do and go for it.

QUESTIONS TO ASK

- Do I work just to pay the mortgage?
- If the answer to the question above is yes, do I have the determination, drive and guts to do something about it?

QUOTATION 88   # AARON LEVENSTEIN ON UNSEEN STATISTICS

Use this to remind you to be suspicious of all statistics, especially those you want to be true.

Aaron Levenstein (1913–86) was an author and Professor of Business Administration at Baruch College. In one of his most memorable quotations he suggested that:

> Statistics are like a bikini [or a pair of Speedos]. What they reveal is suggestive, but what they conceal is vital.
>
> **Aaron Levenstein**

Basically, he is saying that statistics can be used to confuse and mislead the reader. This was very evident in a national newspaper headline a few years ago that screamed, 'Half of all schools in Britain are below average.'

WHAT TO DO

- Don't accept any set of statistics at face value. Find out how the data was collected and analysed and what alternative interpretations can be placed on it. This will mean talking to whoever prepared the figures. For regular routine reports, you'll have to do this only once and then perhaps every year at a minimum to confirm that nothing has changed in how the data has been compiled. For one-off reports, you'll need to do it every time.

- By interrogating the data in this way, you will understand what the information provided actually means (see Quotation 55) and be able to assess just how much reliance you can place on it. Identify weaknesses in it and have ready-made answers for anyone who claims that you've ignored other interpretations of the data.

QUESTIONS TO ASK

- Do I fully understand all the statistical and financial reports I receive? If not, who can I speak to about them?
- Do I just accept the statistical and financial information I'm given or do I critically evaluate it?

QUOTATION 89 | # DAVID PACKARD ON THE IMPORTANCE OF MARKETING

Use this to remind you that people see you as a representative of your organisation.

David Packard (1912–96) was a Co-founder, with William Hewlett, of Hewlett-Packard and served as President, CEO and Chairman of the company. His experience led him to suggest that:

> Marketing is too important to leave to the marketing department.
>
> **David Packard**

Packard was not suggesting that you should dump your marketing department/team. Rather, he was suggesting that every member of staff had a role to play in it.

WHAT TO DO

- In the age of social media, every member of staff has to realise that their actions can reflect on the organisation and be spread worldwide in less than 24 hours (see Quotation 81).
- Seek to build an organisation where everyone from cleaner to CEO recognises that they are representatives of the company and that how they behave with stakeholders, and even in their private life, can have an impact on how people see and judge the organisation. For example, many years ago I decided never to fly with a particular budget airline because I found the CEO obnoxious and I never have. How many other potential customers did he lose with that one interview?
- Conversely, if an engineer gets cornered at a party about a faulty machine that has just been delivered, they can do the organisation's reputation a world of good by taking the details and trying to sort the issue out for the person – even though it's not their responsibility.

QUESTIONS TO ASK

- What can I and my staff do to promote the organisation and its products?
- Have I and my staff had any training about how to deal with complaints received from the organisation's stakeholders?

QUOTATION 90 # ALAN KAY ON THE VALUE OF FAILURE

Use this to remind you that the best lessons often are learnt through failure.

Alan Kay (b. 1940) is an American computer scientist and winner of the Turing Award. He suggests that:

> If you don't fail 90 per cent of the time, you're not aiming high enough.
>
> **Alan Kay**

WHAT TO DO

■ Adopt the Americans' attitude towards failure. In Britain, failure is seen as shameful. Those that fail seldom return for more ritual humiliation. Yet, in America, failure is seen as a learning opportunity. Indeed, many highly successful entrepreneurs have had two or three failures under their belt before they hit the motherlode.

■ Use your learning journal to analyse your mistakes and failures and identify what you did wrong. Maybe you did nothing wrong and it was events beyond your control that stumped you. Either way, learn from your failures.

■ It's not easy to fulfil your potential, or even come close to it. If you aim to be the best you can be, it's highly likely you will fail. But isn't that infinitely better than never trying or being satisfied with a long list of mediocre achievements (see Quotation 87)?

■ Never take failure personally. It's not a reflection on you or your character. Many famous people failed before they succeeded. Winston Churchill had several huge failures to his name before he became Prime Minister in 1940 and saved both Britain and Europe from Nazi domination.

QUESTIONS TO ASK

- Am I able to brush failure off and move on or do I beat myself up?
- Do I think that I must always succeed for people to like/respect me? If so, which friend or family member did you cease talking to after they failed?

CONCLUSION

Bubbling just outside the Top Ten at number eleven is Alan Kay on the value of failure.

In Section 2, I selected Henry Ford's quotation on the need for self-confidence as my Top Ten entry. I choose Ford's quotation as, without self-confidence, or at least the appearance of self-confidence, it's very difficult to manage or lead people.

It is, perhaps, this fragile self-confidence that makes so many people wary of failure. They fear that even one failure could destroy them for life. So they never take a risk or bet the bank on a great idea. This is unfortunate because we know that most successful entrepreneurs/leaders clocked up one or two failures on their CVs before they succeeded. They have used these failures as valuable learning opportunities and have come back stronger and wiser.

ONE LESSON TO TAKE AWAY
Don't be afraid to fail.

THE TOP TEN MANAGEMENT WISDOM QUOTATIONS

Choosing the Top Ten quotations was a highly subjective exercise. My subjectivity was compounded by my decision to choose only one entry from each section and to exclude all the entries in Section 11 from consideration. Does that mean I'm prejudiced against the number 11 or short entries? Who knows? Who cares? The point is that the list is just a bit of fun.

However, you may like to try it yourself, as it forces you to evaluate each entry. Of course, given your unique circumstances, what's useful to you may be very different from what anyone else would find useful.

Rank	Quotation no.	Quotation	Reason for ranking
1	1	**Peter Drucker:** A business exists to create [and retain] a customer.	Expresses the fundamental purpose of all businesses, as profits flow from customers.
2	14	**Henry Ford:** The man who thinks he can and the one who thinks he can't are both right. Which one are you?	Emphasises that without self-confidence, or the appearance of self-confidence, you can achieve nothing as a manager.
3	25	**Warren Buffet:** Somebody once said that in looking for people to hire, you look for three qualities: integrity, intelligence, and energy. And if they don't have the first, the other two will kill you. You think about it; it's true. If you hire somebody without integrity, you really [do] want them to be dumb and lazy.	Tells you what to look for when recruiting staff and reminds you that while staff are potentially your greatest asset, bad staff can destroy your career and the organisation.
4	33	**Warren Bennis:** The most dangerous leadership myth is that leaders are born . . . The myth asserts that people simply either have certain charismatic qualities or not. That's nonsense . . . Leaders are made rather than born.	Challenges the myth that managers are born and not made. It also reminds us that many years ago we stopped believing that by dint of birth the aristocracy are meant to rule over us.
5	77	**Dale Carnegie:** You can close more business in two months by becoming interested in other people than you can in two years by trying to get people interested in you.	Reminds you that too often an over-developed ego can get in the way of effective decision making, management, planning and the job of making sales.
6	75	**Sophocles:** Never command what you cannot enforce... **Rosabeth Moss Kanter:** Power is the ability to get things done.	Outlines the quickest way possible to lose any power you have by showing your inability to get things done.

Rank	Quotation no.	Quotation	Reason for ranking
7	45	**Fredrick Herzberg:** True motivation comes from achievement, personal development, job satisfaction and recognition.	Reminds you that motivation is not about pay and conditions.
8	53	**Mary Parker Follet:** We should never allow ourselves to be bullied by an either-or. There is often the possibility of something better than either of these two alternatives.	A warning to you to avoid assuming that you have only two choices to choose from.
9	61	**Niccolò Machiavelli:** The reformer has enemies in all who profit by the old order, and only lukewarm defenders in those who would profit by the new order.	A warning to you to think through a strategy for how to deal with those who benefit from seeing your change fail.
10	69	**Winston Churchill:** However beautiful the strategy, you should occasionally look at the results.	A reminder to always evaluate the strategy you used. Even if it has been successful, there may have been better options.

And finally, my own personal favourite quotation in the book is from the king himself:

Ambition is a dream with a V8 engine.

Elvis Presley

What a great image it conjures up – and I don't even like *Top Gear!*

RECOMMENDED READING

Basic Books (2003) *The Big Book of Business Quotations.* Bloomsbury Publishing: London.

Goodman, T. (1999) *The Forbes Book of Business Quotations*. Black Dog and Leventhal Publishers: New York.

Ridgers, B. (ed.) (2012) *The Economist's Book of Business Quotations.* The Economist/Profile Books: London.

WEBSITES

If you google 'management quotations' you'll be inundated with hundreds of responses. The four sites listed below are those that I found most useful.

- Brainyquote.com
- Goodreads.com/quotes
- Searchquotes.com
- Thinkexist.com

Remember to use a range of search terms when looking for management quotations. In addition to 'managers'/'management' try 'leaders'/'leadership', 'motivation', 'change management', 'decision making', 'business planning', etc.

LIST OF CONTRIBUTORS

The table below summarises the number of quotations I have used from each person represented. Peter Drucker leads the way with eight. This reflects two things about him. First, he was the pre-eminent commentator on management of the twentieth century and, second, his output over seven decades of work was astonishing.

Names in alphabetical order	Number of quotations	Quotation no.
Adams, John Quincy	1	42
Bennis, Warren	5	10, 33, 36, 55, 82
Blanchard, Kenneth	1	51
Blanchard, Kenneth and Blanchard, S.	1	44
Bower, Marvin	1	3
Bozos, Jeff	2	7, 81
Buckingham, Marcus	1	26
Buffet, Warren	2	25, 80
Burke, Edmund	1	66
Carnegie, Andrew	3	5, 16, 19
Carnegie, Dale	2	13, 77
Chakraborty, S.K.	1	39
Churchill, Winston	1	69
Christensen, Clayton M.	1	76
Deming, Edward	1	37
Dennis, Ron	1	31
Drucker, Peter	8	1, 22, 23, 35, 56, 59, 63, 86
Drummond, Helga	1	50
Edison, Thomas	2	17, 20

(Continued)

Names in alphabetical order	Number of quotations	Quotation no.
Einstein, Albert	1	74
Eisenhower, Dwight D.	1	64
Ford, Henry	2	12, 14
French, John Jr and Raven, Bertram	1	71
Frost, Robert	1	43
Gates, Bill	1	78
Geneen, Harold	1	4
Godin, Seth	1	62
Grove, Andrew S.	1	65
Hadfield, Bud	1	52
Hamel, Gary	1	57
Hammer, Michael and Champy, James	1	58
Handy, Charles	1	21
Herzberg, Fredrick	1	45
Hock, Dee	1	28
Kay, Alan	1	90
Kearns Goodwin, Doris	1	41
Kotler, Philip	1	8
Levenstein, Aaron	1	88
Levitt, Theodore	1	11
Machiavelli, Niccolò	2	61, 73
Maslow, Abraham	1	87
Mintzberg, Henry	1	38
Morgan, John Pierpont	1	85
Moss Kanter, Rosabeth	1	54
Moss Kanter, Rosabeth and Sophocles	1	75
Packard, David	1	89

Names in alphabetical order	Number of quotations	Quotation no.
Parker Follet, Mary	1	53
Patton, General George	1	47
Peter, Laurence J.	1	9
Peters, Tom	2	46, 79
Porter, Michael E.	1	68
Roosevelt, Theodore	1	27
Presley, Elvis	1	83
Sargent, Molly	1	15
Schultz, Howard D.	1	34
Sharma, Robin	1	72
Shapiro, Eileen C.	1	84
Sloan, Alfred P.	1	29
Taylor, Claude I.	1	40
Townsend, Robert	2	24, 49
Walsh, Jack	2	2, 30
Walton, Sam	1	6
Watkins, Bill	1	18
Weber, Max	1	70
Webster, Daniel	1	60
Wooden, John	1	48
Yorke, James	1	67
Ziglar, Zig	1	32

Number of people with:	
Eight entries	1
Five entries	1
Three entries	1
Two entries	10
One entry	54

INDEX